MONUMENTAL INSCRIPTIONS IN THE LIBRARY OF THE SOCIETY OF GENEALOGISTS

PART II
NORTHERN ENGLAND WALES, SCOTLAND, IRELAND, and OVERSEAS

EDITED BY
LYDIA COLLINS
and **MABEL MORTON**

1987

Published by
The Society of Genealogists
14 Charterhouse Buildings
London EC1M 7BA

© Society of Genealogists 1987

ISBN 0 901878 86 3

Printed by St. Richard's Press Ltd.,
Chichester, West Sussex.

CONTENTS

INTRODUCTION

The first thing which must be said about this catalogue, and which cannot be emphasised too strongly, is that it is not intended to indicate to those contemplating the copying of monumental inscriptions that any place included has been completely and exhaustively copied and need not therefore receive their attention. The aim of the work is to indicate to those undertaking research that there exists some kind of copy, however incomplete, for that particular place.

The work begins with a very brief general section and has then been arranged by county according to the boundaries that existed before the 1974 changes. Counties such as Avon or Merseyside etc. will not therefore appear. The counties begin with a general section which contains works which cover so many parishes that it would be impracticable to itemise them individually, and works of a general nature. There then follow the lists of individual places within the county.

The details given have been kept to a minimum. The dedications of churches have been omitted where these are the ancient parish church unless it seemed that confusion might arise. Covering dates have not been shown, and it should be borne in mind that gravestones did not come into general use until the late seventeenth century although few survive from such an early date. Inscriptions in church interiors may well be earlier, and inscriptions from municipal cemeteries will not begin until the nineteenth century.

The titles of printed works have been cited in full. Manuscript and typescript material has been indicated by MS or TS only, together with the date, and this should be sufficient to identify the correct entry in the Library card catalogue to which reference should always be made when looking for material in the Library. In general, printed works are available for loan, but manuscript and typescript material is not.

Where possible an incomplete copy has been indicated by the word 'extract', but its absence should not be taken to indicate that the copy is complete since in many cases it has been quite impossible to judge whether or not a copy was complete at the time when it was made.

Although this is not a complete bibliography but only a list of copies in the Society's Library, in effect this means that most printed works, particularly those in journals, are included. However, there may be some apparent inconsistencies as a result of the Society's collection of a particular periodical being incomplete, and only copies in those volumes which it possesses can be included.

A work of this kind could never have been accomplished without the help of a great number of people, and the following have given valuable assistance in compiling the lists for the various counties: Lionel Aird (Durham, Northumberland), Robert Borland (Scotland), Miss Alison Carpenter (Wales), Miss Stella Colwell (Yorkshire), Miss Anne Patrick (Leicestershire, Lincolnshire), the late Miss J. Edith Pritchard (Herefordshire, Worcestershire), Mrs. Doreen Rossiter (Westmorland), Mrs. Mavis Sharp (Lancashire, Nottinghamshire, Rutland, Staffordshire, Warwickshire, Westmorland, Yorkshire, Scotland), Mrs. Margaret Stone (Lancashire), Mrs. Christine Vialls (Cheshire), Miss Eunice Wilson (Cumberland), Michael Wood (Shropshire), and Dr. Patrick Smythe-Wood (Ireland).

References to inscriptions to be found in the older journals have been based partially on information in a card index of monumental inscriptions begun by members of the Society of Genealogists before the last war but not continued, and a topographical index compiled by the late Major J. B. Whitmore and bequeathed by him to the Society.

The lists cover material acquired by the Library up to early 1987.

ABBREVIATIONS

Beazley's Owen MSS	Partial copy of Owen Manuscripts for the Wirral by F. C. Beazley (1929) MS. Original in Manchester Reference Library
B.g.	burial ground
Bye-gones	column on antiquarian subjects relating to Wales and the Borders published in *The Oswestry Advertizer*
Cath Rec Soc	*Catholic Record Society*
Ch	church
Chap	chapel
Chyd	churchyard
Cmy	cemetery
Coll Top et Gen	*Collectanea Topographica et Genealogica*
Earwaker	*East Cheshire: Past and Present; or a History of the Hundred of Macclesfield* by J. P. Earwaker (1877-80) 2 vols.
extr	extracts
F.H.S.	Family History Society
FL	*Family Links* (Magazine of the Irish Genealogical Association)
Frag Gen	*Fragmenta Genealogica* by F. A. Crisp, vols. 5, 7-13 (1900-09)
Gen	*The Genealogist*
Gen Mag	*Genealogists' Magazine*
Gent Mag	*Gentleman's Magazine*
Hearne	*Remarks and Collections of Thomas Hearne 1705-1735* by C. E. Doble et al (Oxford Historical Society, 1885-1921) 11 vols.
Her & Gen	*Herald and Genealogist*
Here Coll	*Herefordshire Collectanea* by J. H. Bloom, vol. 1 (pre-1927) MS
IA	*Irish Ancestor*
IG	*Irish Genealogist*
MIAu	*Monumental Inscriptions in Australia* (1913-22) 4 vols., MS
Memorials of the Dead	*Journal of the Society for Preserving Memorials of the Dead of Great Britain*
Mfche	microfiche
MG	*Manchester Genealogist*
Misc Gen et Her	*Miscellanea Genealogica et Heraldica*
Mont Coll	*Montgomeryshire Collections*
Moray	*History of the Province of Moray* by L. Shaw (1882) 2 vols.
MS	manuscript
n.d.	no date
N & Q	*Notes and Queries*
Notts FHS RS	*Nottinghamshire Family History Society, Record Series*
SAS	*Transactions of the Shropshire Archaeological Society*
Shears	*Miscellaneous M.I.* by E. J. Shears (1942) TS, from Berks, Bucks, Cambs, Cornwall, Middx and Yorks
Snell	*Genealogical Collections* by F. S. Snell (1883-1909) MS & TS vols.
Top	*The Topographer*
Top & Gen	*Topographer and Genealogist*
TS	typescript
YOM	*Ye Olde Mortality* by A. Weight Matthews, vols. 1-31 & misc vol. (c. 1900-20) MS

GENERAL

Sepulchral Monuments in Great Britain by Richard Gough. *Part I containing the Four First Centuries* (1786); *Part II containing the Fifteenth Century* (1796). Effigies and inscriptions of eminent people who died prior to 1500

Monumenta Anglicana: being inscriptions on the Monuments of several Eminent Persons deceased in or since the Year 1650, to the end of the Year 1679 by John le Neve (1718)

Monumenta Anglicana: . . . Persons deceased in or since the Year 1700, to the end of the Year 1715 by John le Neve (1717)

List of Monumental Brasses in the British Isles by Mill Stephenson (1926). *Appendix to a List of Monumental Brasses in the British Isles* by Mill Stephenson (1938). All known brasses in England, Wales, Scotland, Ireland, museums and private possession

CHESHIRE

The History of Cheshire by G. Ormerod (1882) 3 vols. Mainly church interiors in about half the parishes in the county

Monumental & Other Inscriptions in the Wirral by F. C. Beazley (1903-1907) MS, 3 Vols. Every inscription inside churches in the Wirral and all such inscriptions in the churchyards as were ancient, notable or decaying

"Wirral Records of the 17th Century" by F. C. Beazley in *Transactions of Historic Soc of Lancashire & Cheshire* 77 (1926)

"Calendar of Monumental Inscriptions, Wills, Administrations, etc." by F. C. Beazley in *Lancs & Cheshire Record Soc* 76 (1922)

"Monumental Inscriptions to Cheshire Folk in the Parish Church of Our Lady & St. Nicholas, Liverpool" in *The Cheshire Sheaf* 3 ser xxiii (1926) 75-76

ACTON Ch *Cheshire Sheaf* 3 ser i (1896) 76-78
ALDERLEY Ch Earwaker 2 (1880) 20-21
ALSAGER Ch & Chyd TS (1970)
ASHTON ON MERSEY Ch & extr Chyd *History of the Church of St Martin at Ashton-on-Mersey* by C. J. Renshaw (1914) 6-9 21-22
AUDLEM Ch & Chyd extr *Cheshire Sheaf* 3 ser xxix (1934) 78-79

BACKFORD Ch *Cheshire Sheaf* 3 ser vii (1909) 81 (corrects Ormerod); *Transactions of Historic Soc of Lancashire & Cheshire* 21 (1905) 148-165, also reprinted as a separate volume. Chyd Beazley's Owen MSS (1861)
BARROW, GREAT Ch TS (1951)
BARTHOMLEY Ch & Chyd TS (1970)
BEBINGTON Ch *Cheshire Sheaf* 3 ser vii (1909) 88 (corrects Ormerod); TS (1982). Chyd TS (1970)
BIDSTON Ch Beazley's Owen MSS (1860); *Transactions of Historic Soc of Lancashire & Cheshire* 88 (1936) 36-45
BIRKENHEAD St Mary Ch & Chyd TS (1980). All Saints Ch TS (1972)
BROMBOROUGH Ch *Cheshire Sheaf* 3 ser xxvii (1930) 25 30 32 34 39 41 43-45
BUNBURY Ch & Chyd *Monuments at Bunbury Church* by J. P. Rylands & F. C. Beazley (1918)
BURTON Ch & Chyd Beazley's Owen MSS (c. 1860); *Transactions of Historic Soc of Lancashire & Cheshire* 23 (1907) 11-15 43-46, also reprinted as a separate volume
CARRINGTON Chyd *Manchester Genealogist* 13:3 (1977) 69-72; 13:4 (1977) 99-101
CHADKIRK Ch Earwaker 2 (1880) 83
CHEADLE Ch Earwaker 1 (1877) 213-216
CHELFORD Chyd Earwaker 2 (1880) 368 (1 only)
CHESTER Holy Trinity Ch TS (1970). St Bridget Chyd Xerox of *Chester Archaeological Soc Journal* 51 (1964). St John the Baptist Ch & Chyd TS (1912). St Mary-on-the-Hill Ch & Chyd *St Mary-on-the-Hill* by J. P. Earwaker (1898) 39-76. St Michael Ch *Cheshire Sheaf* 3 ser xxx (1935) 79 80 83 89 91 97
CHURCH MINSHULL Ch *Cheshire Sheaf* 3 ser xxxii (1937) 89 93 105 111 113
CONGLETON St Peter Chyd TS (1986)
DISLEY Ch & Chyd Earwaker 2 (1880) 96-97. Chyd MS (1915)
EASTHAM Ch Beazley's Owen MSS (c. 1860); *Cheshire Sheaf* 3 ser vii (1909) 86 (corrects Ormerod). Ch & Chyd *Cheshire Sheaf* 3 ser x (1914) 65-67 70 71-74 76 78 80-81 85-87 89-90 92-94 97 99-100 102 105-106 108-109 111 114-115 117 120. Chyd TS (1981)
GAWSWORTH Ch *Transactions of the Ancient Monuments Soc* NS 5 (1957) 79-147. Ch & Chyd Earwaker 2 (1880) 581-586
GRAPPENHALL Chyd *Top & Gen* 1 (1846) 464-465; *Cheshire Sheaf* 3 ser xiii (1916) 68 71 73 76 78 81 84
HEATON NORRIS See LANCASHIRE
HESWALL Ch Beazley's Owen MSS (c. 1860); *Cheshire Sheaf* 3 ser vii (1909) 90 (corrects

Ormerod); *Heswall Parish Church* by T. H.
May (1921) 25-28

HYDE Ch & Chyd *History of Hyde Chapel* by
J. Thornely & T. Middleton (1908) 49-50 108-
113. Cmy TS (1950)

KIRBY, WEST Ch Beazley's Owen MSS (n.d.)

KNUTSFORD Norbury Boothes B.g. *Lancs &
Cheshire Historian* 1 (1965) 81-82 107-108
129-130

LYME HANDLEY Plague B.g. MS (1973)

MACCLESFIELD St Michael Ch Earwaker 2
(1880) 491-501; Chyd TS (1979). Roe Street
Congregational B.g. TS (1983). Forest Chap &
B.g. TS (1981)

MARBURY Ch *Cheshire Sheaf* 3 ser ii (1898)
9-11

MARPLE Ch Earwaker 2 (1880) 56

MARTON Chyd TS (1984)

MIDDLEWICH Ch *Cheshire Notes & Queries*
5 (1900) 31-32

MOBBERLEY Knolls Green Friends B.g. *Lancs
& Cheshire Historian* 2 (1966) 253-254 314
377

MOTTRAM IN LONGDENDALE Ch & Chyd
Earwaker 2 (1880) 122-124

NANTWICH Ch *The History of Nantwich* by J.
Hall (1883) 310-327

NESTON Ch *Cheshire Sheaf* 3 ser vii (1909) 91
(corrects Ormerod). Ch & Chyd Beazley's
Owen MSS (c. 1860). Chyd TS (1970)

NEWBOLD ASTBURY Chyd *Cheshire Sheaf*
3 ser xxxi (1936) 101 103 105-107

NORTHENDEN Ch & Chyd Earwaker 1 (1877)
281-286; TS (1970)

OVER Chyd TS (1986); index *Cheshire F.H.S.
Journal* 6:4 (1977) 18-19

OVERCHURCH Chyd Beazley's Owen MSS (c.
1860)

PLEMSTALL Ch *Cheshire Sheaf* 3 ser x (1913)
24 26 28-29 31 33 35 37 38-39

POTT SHRIGLEY Ch Earwaker 2 (1880) 329-
330. Chyd TS (1983)

PRESTBURY Ch *Chetham Soc* 97 (1876) 30-
39. Ch & Chyd Earwaker 2 (1880) 197-203

RAINOW Ch & Chyd TS (1983). Methodist
B.g. TS (1981). Hough Hole House B.g. TS
(1982)

SALE Cmy *Manchester Genealogist* 15 (1978-
1979) 21

SALTERSFORD Jenkin Chapel B.g. TS (1980)

SHOTWICK Ch *Cheshire Sheaf* 3 ser vii (1909)
91 (corrects Ormerod). Ch & Chyd Beazley's
Owen MSS (c 1880); *Notes on Shotwick* by F.
C. Beazley (1915) 30-41 122-133

STOAK Ch *Cheshire Sheaf* 3 ser vii (1909) 84
(corrects Ormerod). Ch & Chyd *Transactions
of Historic Soc of Lancashire & Cheshire* 21

(1905) 128-147, also reprinted as a separate
volume

STOCKPORT St Mary Ch Earwaker 1 (1877)
368-377

TAXALL Ch Earwaker 2 (1880) 542-543

THELWALL *Top & Gen* 1 (1846) 463-464

THORNTON-LE-MOORS Ch Beazley's Owen
MSS (c. 1860). Ch & Chyd *Transaction of
Historic Soc of Lancashire & Cheshire* 21
(1905) 166-194, also reprinted as a separate
volume

THURSTASTON Ch *Cheshire Sheaf* 3 ser vii
(1909) 90 (corrects Ormerod); Beazley's Owen
MSS (c. 1860). Ch & Chyd *Thurstaston* by F.
C. Beazley (1924) 102 110 112-117

TINTWHISTLE Ebenezer Weslyan B.g. TS
(1981)

UPTON-IN-OVERCHURCH Chyd Beazley's
Owen MSS (c. 1860)

WALLASEY Withens Lane Friends B.g.
Cheshire F.H.S. Journal 12:1 (1982) 13-15

WAVERTON Ch TS (1904); *Cheshire Sheaf*
3 ser xx (1923) 67-68 70

WEAVERHAM Chyd extr *North Cheshire
Family Historian* 5:2 (1978) 46

WILMSLOW Earwaker 1 (1877) 82-85

WOODCHURCH Ch *Cheshire Sheaf* 3 ser vii
(1909) 90 (corrects Ormerod). Ch & Chyd
*Transactions of Historic Soc of Lancashire &
Cheshire* 17 (1901) 167-178. Chyd Beazley's
Owen MSS (c. 1860)

WYBUNBURY Ch *Cheshire Sheaf* 3 ser xxxii
(1937) 41 42 45 54 58 60-61 65

CUMBERLAND

"Busts, Portrait Medallions & Modern Effigies
in the Churches of the Diocese of Carlisle" by
the Rev. R. Bower in *Transactions of the
Cumberland & Westmorland Antiquarian &
Archaeological Soc.* NS 4 (1904) 118-145

*A History of the Churches of the Rural Deanery
of Whitehaven* by Caesar Caine (1916). Most
churches & a few from churchyards of
Arlecdon, Bigrigg, Cleator, Cleator Moor,
Distington, Egremont, Frizington, Harrington,
Hensingham, Lamplugh, Moresby, St Bees,
Whitehaven — Christ Church, Holy Trinity,
St James, St Nicholas

ALSTON Chyd MS of parish register (1941)

BEWCASTLE Chyd TS (1973)

BRIDEKIRK Ch & Chyd *The Monumental
Inscriptions of Brigham & Bridekirk* by H. T.
Wake (1878) 59-104

BRIGHAM Chyd *The Monumental Inscriptions of Brigham & Bridekirk* by H. T. Wake (1878) 1-58

CARLISLE Ch & Chyd *The Monumental Inscriptions in the Church & Churchyard of St Cuthbert, Carlisle* by M. J. Ferguson (1889). Chyd TS (1977)

CLEATOR Ch & Chyd *Pre-1900 Memorial Inscriptions of Haile Church & St Leonard, Cleator* (Cumbria F.H.S. 1985)

CROSS CANONBY Ch & Chyd *Monumental Inscriptions of Crosscanonby* (Cumbria F.H.S. 1983)

CROSTHWAITE Ch & (extr) Chyd *The Parish Church of St Kentigern, Crosthwaite* by F. C. Eeles (1953) 18 21 28 35-40 71-76

DALSTON Ch, Chyd & Cmy *The Monumental Inscriptions of the Church, Churchyard & Cemetery of St Michael's, Dalston* by J. Wilson (1890)

GARRIGILL Chyd TS of parish register (1908)

HAILE Ch & Chyd *Pre-1900 Memorial Inscriptions of Haile Church & St Leonard, Cleator* (Cumbria F.H.S. 1985)

KIRK ANDREWS ON ESK Chyd TS (1973)

MARYPORT Chyd (maritime memorials) *Cumbria F.H.S. Newsletter* 20 (1981) 22-23; 21 (1981) 19-20; 22 (1982) 18-20

REDWING Nonconformist B.g. TS (n.d.)

ROCKCLIFFE WITH CARGO Chyd TS (1981)

STAPLETON Ch & Chyd TS (1974)

SUNBRICK Friends B.g. *Transactions of the Cumberland & Westmorland Antiquarian & Archaeological Soc.* NS 6 (1906) 275-278

SWARTHMOOR Friends B.g. *Transactions of the Cumberland & Westmorland Antiquarian & Archaeological Soc.* NS 6 (1906) 280-283

WHITEHAVEN Ch & Chyd *Monumental Inscriptions of the Church & Churchyard of St James, Whitehaven* by H. B. Stout (1963)

WYTHBURN Chyd TS (1963)

DERBYSHIRE

S. Glover, *The History and Gazetteer of the County of Derby* Vol. II, Part I (1833) monuments in churches in almost every parish from A to Derby. Continuation volume edited by Derbyshire Archaeological Society (1956) covers Doveridge to Eyam

Monumental Inscriptions by White Watson (1806) MS. Extracts from Ashford Ch, Bakewell Ch & Chyd, Barlow Chapel Ch, Beeley Ch, Bolsover Ch, Bonsal Ch, Bradley Ch, Breadsall Ch, Darley Ch, Dronfield Ch & Chyd, Eckington Ch, Fenny Bentley Ch, Hartington Ch, Heanor Ch & Chyd, Ilkeston Chyd, Monyash Ch, Morley Chyd, Morton Ch, Staveley Ch, Stony Middleton Ch, Tideswell Ch, West Hallam Ch, Youlgreave Ch

Haydn Whitehead Card Index: MIs from various parishes arranged alphabetically by surname

ALKMONTON Ch & Chyd TS (1981)

ALSOP EN LE DALE Ch & Chyd TS (1981)

ASHBOURNE Ch *A Guide to Ashbourne Parish Church* by E. A. Sadler (1934) *passim.* Chyd TS (1958)

ASHOVER Ch *The Saints and Sinners of Ashover* by C. E. L. (1924) 22-26; extr *Gent Mag* (1791) II, 790 998

ATLOW Ch & Chyd TS (1982)

BAKEWELL Ch & Chyd extr *Some Interesting and Unusual Inscriptions in All Saints Church and Churchyard, Bakewell* by R. W. P. Cockerton (2nd edn, 1957)

BARROW ON TRENT Cmy TS (1961) (opened 1928)

BELPER Ch & Chyd TS (1978); *Branch News* 15 (Dec 1980) 10-11. Chapel Street Wesleyan B.g. TS (1983)

BLACKWELL Newton Old Hall *Branch News* 21 (June 1982) 15

BOLSOVER Congregational B.g. TS (1981)

BOYLESTONE Ch *Gent Mag* (1792) II, 884-885 (Allsop family); *Branch News* 12 (Mar 1980) 12-13. Ch & Chyd TS (1981). Chyd *Branch News* 11 (Dec 1979) 10-14

BRIMINGTON Chyd list, cutting from *Derbyshire Times* 4 Jan 1974

CALKE Ch & Chyd TS (1985)

CHESTERFIELD Ch *Top* 3 (1790) 335-338; *Gent Mag* (1793) II, 977; (1794) I, 15-17

CHURCH GRESLEY Chyd TS (1980)

CODNOR Ch & Chyd TS (1978)

CRICH Ch *Coll Top et Gen* 1 (1834) 42-51

CUBLEY Ch & Chyd TS (1980)

DALBURY Ch & Chyd TS (1978); *Branch News* 4 (Mar 1978) 7-11

DERBY Christ Church Ch TS (1980). Holy Trinity Ch & Chyd TS (1979). St Alkmund Ch & Chyd TS (c 1974). St Anne Ch TS (1981). St Barnabas Ch TS (1981). St James the Greater Ch TS (1981-82). St James the Less Chyd TS (1979). St John the Evangelist Ch TS (1979). St Luke Ch TS (1981). St Michael Ch & Chyd TS (1979); *Branch News* 16 (Mar 1981) 8-11. St Paul Ch & Chyd TS (1981). St Peter Ch & Chyd TS (1979). St Werburg Ch & Chyd TS

(1978). Agard Street Particular Baptist Chap Glover, *op. cit.*; B.g. TS (1980). Brook Street Baptist Chap Glover, *op. cit.* Friar Gate Unitarian Chap Glover, *op. cit.*

DUFFIELD General Baptist Chap & B.g. TS (1981)

ERRWOOD HALL (near BUXTON) Private B.g. TS (c 1979); *Branch News* 10 (1979) 10

EYAM Ch & extr Chyd *History and Antiquities of Eyam* by W. Wood (1865) 161-163 167-175

GLOSSOP Ch & Chyd TS (1978)

HAZELWOOD Ch & Chyd TS (1981)

HEANOR Ch & Chyd TS (1978); *Branch News* 5 (June 1978) 8-11; 6 (Sept 1978) 9-11; 7 (Dec 1978) 7-10

HEATH Old Chyd TS (1982)

HOGNASTON Ch & Chyd TS (1983)

HORSLEY Chyd TS (1961)

HUCKLOW, GREAT Unitarian B.g. TS (1982). Methodist Chapel TS (1982)

IRONVILLE Ch & Chyd TS (1981)

KEDLESTON Ch & Chyd TS (1980)

KING STERNDALE Ch & Chyd TS (1982)

KIRK HALLAM Chyd TS (1960-61)

KIRK IRETON Chyd TS (1976)

LANGLEY MILL Central Baptist B.g. TS (1983)

LONG EATON Mount Tabor Methodist B.g. (now in Cmy) TS (1982)

LONGFORD Ch (Coke family) *Frag Gen* 7 (1902) 42-43. Cmy TS (1980) (opened 1920)

LONG LANE Ch & Chyd TS (1978); *Branch News* 13 (June 1980) 10-13

LONGSTONE, LITTLE Independent Chapel Porch & B.g. TS (1981)

MACKWORTH Ch & Chyd TS (1977); TS (n.d.)

MELBOURNE Ch *The History of Melbourne* by J. J. Briggs (1853) 177-184; *Branch News* 9 (June 1979) 12-15. New Jerusalem Chap TS (1982). Church Street R.C. Ch TS (1983). High Street Congregational Chap TS (1983)

MUGGINTON Ch & Chyd TS (1981)

NEWTON see BLACKWELL

NORBURY Ch *Top* 2 (1790) 231-234

NORMANTON BY DERBY Ch & Chyd TS (n.d.)

PENTRICH Ch & Chyd TS (1978); *Branch News* 1 (Aug 1976) 8; 2 (June 1977) 6-9; 3 (Nov 1977) 8-18

PINXTON Chyd TS (1980) copied 1922

QUARNDON Old Church Chyd TS (1977); *Branch News* 14 (Sept 1980) 10-12. St Paul Ch & Chyd TS (1978)

RADBOURNE Ch & Chyd TS (1978)

REPTON Ch *Top* 2 (1790) 282. Ch & (extr)

Chyd *History of Repton* by R. Bigsby (1854) 129-142 151

SANDIACRE Ch & Chyd *Nottinghamshire F.H.S. Records Series* 13 (1981) 31-48

SHIRLEY Ch & Chyd TS (1980)

SMALLEY Ch *Smalley, Its History and Legends* by C. Kerry (1905) 33-34

SMISBY Ch extr *Misc Gen et Her* 4 ser v (1914) 39

SPONDON Ch, Chyd and Chapel Street B.g. TS (1978)

STAVELEY Ch *Coll Top et Gen* 1 (1834) 36-42; *Gent Mag* (1820) II, 577-580

SUDBURY Ch *Top* 2 (1790) 218-224

SUTTON ON THE HILL Ch & Chyd TS (1980)

SWADLINCOTE Ch & Chyd TS (1981)

SWANWICK Ch & Chyd TS (1974). Chyd Index TS (1977)

TAXALL see CHESHIRE

TIDESWELL Ch extr *A Guide to Tideswell and its Church* by J. M. J. Fletcher (n.d.) *passim;* extr *Gent Mag* (1794) II, 1101-1102

TOADHOLE FURNESS Quaker B.g. TS (1984)

TRUSLEY Ch & Chyd TS (1980); Chyd TS (1980)

TURNDITCH Ch & Chyd TS (1981)

WESSINGTON Ch & Chyd TS (1983)

DURHAM

History and Antiquities of the County Palatinate of Durham by R. Surtees (1816-1840) 4 vols. Extrs from churches and churchyards throughout county

Durham M.I. MS (n.d.). Extracts from Boldon, Durham St Mary the Less, Gainford, Gateshead St Mary, Lamesley, Muggleswick, South Shields Holy Trinity, Stockton, Westoe, and possibly elsewhere

BARNARD CASTLE Chyd *Teesdale Record Soc* 5 (1939-40) 8-16 (copied 1841-43)

BISHOP WEARMOUTH Chyd TS (1903)

BOLDON, WEST Chyd TS (1976)

BRANCEPATH Chyd TS (1977)

CASTLE EDEN Chyd TS (1979)

CHESTER LE STREET Chyd TS (1946)

DALTON LE DALE Chyd TS (1979)

DINSDALE Ch & Chyd TS (1977)

DURHAM Cathedral Ch & Chyd *The Monumental Inscriptions of the Cathedral, Parish Churches, and Cemeteries of the City of Durham* by C. M. Carlton (1880) 3-80. St

Giles Ch & Chyd R.C. memorials TS (n.d.). St
Mary the Less Ch & Chyd C. M. Carlton, *op.
cit.* 83-103. St Mary le Bow Ch & Chyd C. M.
Carlton, *op. cit.* 107-116. North and South
Bailey Cmy C. M. Carlton, *op. cit.* 119-132. St
Oswald Ch & Chyd C. M. Carlton, *op. cit.*
135-312; R. C. memorials TS (n.d.)
EASINGTON Chyd TS (1978)
EGGLESCLIFFE Ch & Chyd TS (1975)
ELDON Chyd TS (1980/81)
ELTON Chyd TS (1976)
HARTLEPOOL Chyd TS of parish register vol.
3 (1968) 267-361
HAUGHTON LE SKERNE Ch & Chyd TS
(1977)
HAVERTON HILL Chyd TS (1976)
HEATHERYCLEUGH Chyd TS (1978)
HUNSTANWORTH Chyd "Some Durham
Parishes": volume of cuttings from *The
Durham County Advertiser* (c. 1908) p. 19
HURWORTH Ch & Chyd TS (1977)
LONG NEWTON Chyd TS (1976)
MIDDLETON ST GEORGE Ch & Chyd TS
(1977)
MONKWEARMOUTH Chyd extr *Journal of
Northumberland and Durham F.H.S.* 4:4
(July 1979) 117
MUGGLESWICK Ch & Chyd *The Parish
Registers of Muggleswick from 1784 to 1812*
by J. W. Fawcett (1906) 52-66
PENSHAW Chyd MS (1976)
RYHOPE Chyd TS (1976)
RYTON Ch & Chyd TS (1976)
SADBERGE Chyd TS (1976) (includes copy
taken 1832)
SATLEY Chyd *The Parish Registers of St.
Cuthbert's Church, Satley from 1560 to 1812*
by J. W. Fawcett (n.d.) 139-152
SHILDON Chyd TS (1976)
SOUTHWICK Ch TS (n.d.)
TANFIELD Ch & Chyd TS (1974)
WASHINGTON Chyd TS (1976)
WOLSINGHAM Chyd MS (n.d.)

HEREFORDSHIRE

ABBEY DORE Ch *Gen* NS 30 (1914) 29-34
128-134 174-181 213-218; bound offprint
ALMELEY Chyd *Here Coll* 1
ASHPERTON Chyd MS (1914)
BISHOPS FROME Chyd *Here Coll* 1
BISHOPTON Chyd *Here Coll* 1
BREDENBURY Ch *Here Coll* 1
BREDWARDINE Chyd *Here Coll* 1
BRIDGE SOLLARS Chyd MS (1914)

BRILLEY Chyd MS (n.d.)
BROBURY Chyd *Here Coll* 1
BROMYARD Chyd *Here Coll* 1
BUCKNELL Chyd *Here Coll* 1
BURRINGTON Chyd *Here Coll* 1
BYFORD Chyd *Here Coll* 1
CLEHONGER Chyd *Here Coll* 1; MS (1914)
COLLINGTON Chyd *Here Coll* 1
DOCKLOW Chyd *Here Coll* 1
DONNINGTON Chyd TS (1947)
DORMINGTON Ch *Here Coll* 1
DOWNTON Chyd *Here Coll* 1
EATON BISHOP Chyd MS (1914)
EYE Chyd MS (1914)
FELTON Chyd *Here Coll* 1
GOODRICH Chyd *Cath Rec Soc* 12 (1913)
263-264
GRENDON BISHOP Chyd *Here Coll* 1
HAMPTON BISHOP Chyd *Here Coll* 1
HEREFORD Cathedral *Monumental
Inscriptions in the Cathedral Church of
Hereford* by F. T. Havergal (1881);
*Transactions of the Bristol & Gloucester
Archaeological Soc* 27 (1904) 26-27;
*Monumental Brasses in the Cathedral Church
of Hereford* by the Ven A. G. Winnington-
Ingham (1956). St Owen Chyd MS (1914)
KIMBOLTON Chyd MS (1914)
KINGSLAND Ch *Gent Mag* (1826) II 583;
(1840) II 259
KINGTON Ch *Gent Mag* (1846) II 525. Ch &
Chyd TS (1986)
LEDBURY Ch *Gent Mag* (1793) II 911
LLANGARREN Chyd *Cath Rec Soc* 12 (1913)
262-263
MARDEN Ch *Gen* 7 (1883) 233-234
MUNSLEY Ch *Registers of Munsley* by Rev
M. Hopton (1903) vii-viii
OCLE PYCHARD Chyd MS (1914)
PUDLESTON Chyd MS (1914)
RICHARDS CASTLE see SHROPSHIRE
ROSS Chyd *Cath Rec Soc* 12 (1913) 262
ST DEVEREUX Ch & Chyd MS (n.d.)
SARNESFIELD Chyd *Gen* NS 12 (c. 1895) 7-8
SUTTON ST MICHAEL Ch *Gen* 7 (1883)
234-235
TEDSTONE DELAMERE Ch *Gent Mag*
(1811) I 429-430
THRUXTON Chyd MS (1914)
UPTON BISHOP Ch & Chyd *Records of
Upton Bishop* by F. T. Havergal (1883) 42-54
WALTERSTONE Ch *Misc Gen et Her* 5 ser iii
(1918-19) 248-250
WELSH BICKNOR Chyd *Cath Rec Soc* 12
(1913) 265-266
WELSH NEWTON Chyd *Cath Rec Soc* 12
(1913) 236- 238

WESTHIDE Chyd MS (1914)
WESTON BEGGARD Chyd MS (1914)
WHITNEY Ch MS (n.d.)
YARKHILL Chyd MS (1914)

LANCASHIRE

The History of the County Palatine and Duchy of Lancaster by Edward Baines Snr (revised edn 1888-1893) 5 vols. Extract from various church interiors

"Calendar of Monumental Inscriptions, Wills, Administrations, etc." by F. C. Beazley in *Lancs & Cheshire Record Soc* 76 (1922). Name index to MI contained in 162 books in Liverpool Public Reference Library

ASTLEY Chyd *MG* 16:3 (1980) 81; 17:3 (1980) 80-82
ASTLEY BRIDGE Ch & Chyd Mfche (1985)
BARNOLDSWICK Cmy list TS (1982)
BARROWFORD Chyd MS (1973). Higherford Methodist B.g. MS (1973). All Souls R.C. Cmy Mfche (n.d.)
BARTON ON IRWELL R.C. B.g. *MG* 15:2 (1979) 48. Wesleyan Cmy *MG* 14:4 (1978) 103:106
BELMONT Congragational B.g. Mfche (1976)
BELTHORN Independent B.g. Mfche (1983)
BIRCH IN RUSHOLME Chyd extr *MG* 15:3 (1979) 73
BIRCH ST MARY Chyd xerox of TS (1980)
BIRTLE Chyd Mfche (1981)
BLACKBURN Chyd map & list Mfche (1975). B.gs. Islington Particular Baptist, Chapel Street Congregational, Clayton Street Wesleyan Methodist, Feilden Street United Free Methodist Mfche (1983)
BLACKPOOL St John Mfche (1980). Holy Trinity Chyd Mfche (1980). Bethesda B.g. Mfche (1978)
BRIERCLIFFE Ch & Chyd Mfche (1981). Briercliffe Hill B.g. Mfche (copied pre 1859). John Eckroyd's Orchard & Foulds House B.g. Mfche (copied pre 1859). Haggate Baptist B.g. inc Hill Lane Chapel MS (1975); Mfche (1981)
BRIERFIELD Providence Independent Congregational B.g. MS (1972). Primitive Methodist B.g. MS (1972)
BROUGHTON Ch & Chyd *The History of the Parish of Preston* by Henry Fishwick (1900) 138-140
BURNLEY Ch & Chyd extrs *History of the Parochial Church of Burnley* by T. T.

Wilkinson, (1856) 96-104. Holy Trinity, The Mitre Ch & Chyd Mfche (1981). Bethesda Congregational B.g. list TS (1961)
BURTONWOOD Chyd TS (1984)
BURY Holebottom Unitarian B.g. Mfche (1979)
CARTMEL Priory Ch Hearne IV, 16-19; Chyd TS (1983)
CASTLETOWN Ch *Parish Church of St. Mary* by P.G.R. (1926) 38-40
CHEETHAM St Luke Chyd *MG* 13:2 (1977) 42-47; TS (1986)
CHORLEY Ch & extr Chyd *Chorley Church, the Story of the Old Parish Church of Chorley* by J. Wilson (1914) 119-121 147-180
CHORLTON-CUM-HARDY St Clement Ch list TS (1965). St Werburgh Ch list TS (1965)
CHORLTON-ON-MEDLOCK Chyd extr *MG* 15:1 (1979) 9-12
CLAYTON-LE-MOORS St Mary R.C. B.g. Mfche (1982)
COLNE St Bartholomew Ch & Chyd *Annals & Stories of Colne & Neighbourhood* by J. Carr (1878) 133-136 140-143; xerox of MS (1976). Christ Church Chyd MS (1975). Winewall Inghamite Chapel B.g. Mfche (1981). Keighley Road Cmy MS (1978). See also BARROWFORD
COLTON Ch *Colton Registers* ed by A. Anderson Williams & J. Pennington Burns (1891) 265-282
CRAWSHAWBOOTH Rakefoot Methodist B.g. Mfche (n.d.)
CROFT Ch & Chyd TS (1983). St Lewis R.C. B.g. list TS (1972). Lady Lane Unitarian B.g. list TS (1971)
DEANE Ch & Chyd Mfche (1983)
DIDSBURY Ch *Chetham Soc* 42 (1857) 24-29
DOWNHAM Ch & Chyd Mfche (1981)
ECCLES Ch *The Ancient Parish Church of Eccles* by T. D. S. Bayley (1864) 42-46
FARNWORTH Ch *Gent Mag* (1824) II, 198-200
FENCE Chyd Mfche (1981)
FLIXTON Ch & extr Chyd *A History of Flixton, Urmston & Davyhulme* by R. Lawson (1898) 28-30 37-42
FOULRIDGE Friends (New Farm) B.g. Mfche (1982)
GARSTANG Ch & extr Chyd *Chetham Soc* 54 (1878) 93-98
GOOSNARGH Ch & Chyd TS (1966)
HALLIWELL Chyd Mfche (1982)
HAPTON Ch & Chyd Mfche (1982)
HASLINGDEN Chyd Mfche (n.d.)
HASLINGDEN GRANE Chyd Mfche (1980). Methodist B.g. Mfche (1980)
HAWKSHEAD Ch & Chyd *The Monumental*

Inscriptions in the Parish Church & Churchyard of Hawkeshead, Lancs & in the Burial Grounds of Satterthwaite, the Baptists at Hawkeshead Hill, & the Quakers at Colthouse by H. Swainson Cowper (1892)
HEATON NORRIS Chyd TS (1977)
HIGHAM Ch list TS (1980). Wesleyan Chap & B.g. Mfche (n.d.)
HILL-CLIFFE Dissenting Chapel B.g. *Local Gleanings Relating to Lancashire and Cheshire* (1877) 64, repr from *Manchester Courier* 25 May 1877
HINDLEY All Saints Ch *Chetham Soc* NS 18 (1890) 777-778
HODDLESDEN Chyd Mfche (1981)
HOLCOMBE Ch & Chyd extr *The Country and Church of the Cheeryble Brothers* by W. Hume Elliot (1893) 63-68. St Andrew Presbyterian Ch (Grant Family) *ibid* 91-102. Emmanuel Ch & Chyd Mfche (1983)
HOOLE Ch & Chyd Mfche (1982)
HORWICH Chyd Mfche (1985)
HULME Chyd extr *MG* (Spring 1972) 19-20
HURSTWOOD Baptist B.g. Mfche (1981)
KIRKHAM Ch & extr Chyd *Chetham Soc* 92 (1874) 128-134
LADYBURN Ch *St Chad's Church, Ladybarn, Manchester* by E. B. Ward & S. D. Sedgley (1925) 36-39
LANCASTER St Mary Ch *Historic Notes on Lancaster* by Cross Fleury (1891) 6-22; Chyd *Lancs & Cheshire Historian* 1 (1965) 39-40 63-64 85-86 113-116 135-136 161-162 183-186 205-206 231-232; 2 (1966) 257-258 353-358 407-416 477-480; 3:1 (1967) 553-558; xerox of TS (1972). St John Ch Cross Fleury *op cit* 332-335. Presbyterian Chapel, St Nicholas Street Chap & B.g. Cross Fleury *op cit* 363-366
LATCHFORD see WARRINGTON
LEIGH Chyd TS (1937)
LEVENSHULME Wesleyan Chap B.g. (copied 1894) *MG* 14:1 (1978) 17-20
LEVER BRIDGE Ch & Chyd Mfche (1985)
LEYLAND St Andrew Ch list TS (1972). St James Chyd Mfche (1982)
LITTLEBOROUGH Ch *History of the Parish of Rochdale* by H. Fishwick (1889) 193-195
LIVERPOOL St Luke Ch MS (1928). St Nicholas Ch & Chyd *Misc Gen et Her* NS4 (1884) 408-409 429-435. St Oswald R.C. B.g. TS (1939). Unitarian B.g. *Unitarian Chapel, Renshaw Street* by J. Rhind (1903)
LONGSIGHT Chyd extr *MG* 14:3 (1978) 81
LYDIATE Abbey Ch *Gent Mag* (1821) II, 597
MAGHULL Ch & extr Chyd *Transactions of Historic Soc of Lancashire & Cheshire* 74 (1922) 57-59

MANCHESTER St Michael, Angel Street Chyd *MG* 2:1 (1965) 23-24; 2:2 (1966) 23-24. Rusholme Road Cmy *MG* 13:3 (1977) 80
MARSDEN Marsden Heights B.g. Mfche (copied pre 1859). Friends Meeting House B.g. Mfche (1923)
MARSDEN, GREAT Ch & Chyd MS (1973); Mfche (1983)
MARSDEN, LITTLE Ch & Chyd MS (1972)
MEOLS, NORTH Ch & extr Chyd *A History of North Meols* by W. Farrer (1903)
MERE CLOUGH Methodist Mfche (1980)
MILNROW St James Chyd Mfche (n.d.)
MONTON Unitarian B.g. *MG* 17:1 (1981) 19-22; 17:2 (1981) 49-52; 17:3 (1981) 76-79
NEWCHURCH Ch & Chyd TS (1971)
NEW CROSS Ch list TS (1982)
NEWHEAD Friends B.g. Mfche (1982)
NORTHENDEN see CHESHIRE
OGDEN Baptist B.g. TS (1984)
OLDHAM All Saints, Northmoor Old Ch TS (1986). Greenacres Congregational B.g. Mfche (1982)
PADIHAM Ch & Chyd Mfche (1981). Hall Hill Methodist Old B.g. off North Street MS (1951); Mfche (1980). Chapel Walk B.g. Mfche (1980). Nazareth Chapel, West Street B.g. Mfche (n.d.)
PENDLETON All Saints Ch & Chyd Mfche (1982). St. Ann, Brindle Heath Chyd TS (1986). Jewish B.g. TS (1986)
PICKUP BANK Congregational B.g. Mfche (1980)
POULTON-LE-FYLDE Ch & extr Chyd *Chetham Soc* NS 8 (1885) 50-59. Chyd TS (1982)
PRESCOT Chyd index *Liverpool Family Historian* 2:2 (1978) 31-32
PRESTON St George Ch *The History of the Parish of Preston* by H. Fishwick (1900) 153. St John Ch & extr Chyd Fishwick *op cit* 120-124. St Paul Ch & Chyd Mfche (1981). St Saviour Ch Mfche (1984). Corporation Cmy War Graves *Magazine of Rossendale Soc for Lancs* 4:2 (1983) 10-14
RAINFORD Independent B.g. list TS (1974)
READ IN WHALLEY Ch & Chyd Mfche (1981)
RIBCHESTER Ch & Chyd *The History of the Parish of Ribchester* by T. C. Smith & J. Shortt (1890) 205-209
RISLEY Presbyterian Chap & B.g. list TS (1972)
ROCHDALE St Chad Ch & extr Chyd *History of Rochdale* by J. Butterworth (1828) 72-73 76-84; *History of the Parish of Rochdale* by H. Fishwick (1889) 153-163. St Mary, Cheetham

Street Ch & extr Chyd Fishwick *op cit* 217-219. Friends B.g. Mfche (1982)

RUSHOLME Platt Chap & B.g. list TS (1975)

SABDEN St Nicholas, Hey Houses Ch & Chyd Mfche (1981). Baptist B.g. Mfche (1981). Methodist B.g. Mfche (1981)

ST HELENS Chyd list TS (1971). Tontine Street Wesleyan B.g. list *Liverpool Family Historian* 6:3 (1984) 55-56

ST MICHAEL ON WYRE Chyd Mfche (1982)

SANKEY, GREAT Ch & extr Chyd *Lancashire & Cheshire Antiquarian Notes* 1 (1885) 66-67

SEFTON Ch *Gent Mag* (1814) II, 521

SOUTHPORT Chyd list TS (1973)

STANDISH Ch Hearne IV, 14-15

STRETFORD Old Chyd list TS (1968)

TODMORDEN Ch & extr Chyd *History of the Parish of Rochdale* by H. Fishwick (1889) 180

TRAFFORD PARK Ch list TS (1982)

TRAWDEN Chyd Mfche (1981). Wesleyan Methodist Mfche (1980)

ULVERSTON Holy Trinity Ch & extr Chyd TS (1936). St Mary Ch & extr Chyd *The Registers of Ulverston Parish Church* by C. W. Bardsley & L. R. Ayre (1886) lxxxiv-cxi *passim;* TS (1936). Congregational Chap & B.g. TS (1936)

UPHOLLAND Ch & Chyd *Chetham Soc* NS 18 (1890) 745-748

WALMSLEY Chyd Mfche (1984). Unitarian B.g. TS (1982)

WARRINGTON St Elphin Chyd extr *Lancs & Cheshire Notes* 2 (1851) 147-149. St Paul, Bewsey Road Ch & Chyd TS (1982). St James, Latchford Ch & Chyd TS (1979). Friends Meeting House B.g. TS (1979) St Alban R.C. B.g. TS (1979). Unitarian Chap & B.g. *Warrington Unitarian Registers & Memorial Inscriptions* by J. R. Bulmer (1980) 31-48

WAVERTREE Chyd TS (1977); TS (1980)

WERNETH Ch TS (1985)

WHEATLEY CARR Inghamite Church B.g. MS (1974)

WHEATLEY LANE Methodist Chap & B.g. Mfche (1980)

WIGAN Ch *A Ramble Round the Wigan Parish Church* by W. J. True (1901) 70-86. Ch & extr Chyd *Chetham Soc* NS18 (1890) 705-715; Hearne IV, 11-13

WINDLESHAW CHANTRY Chyd TS (1985)

WINWICK Ch & Chyd Hearne IV, 9-11 13-14. Ch, Chyd & New B.g. TS (1971)

WITHINGTON Chyd extr *MG* 15:3 (1979) 71-73

WORSTHORNE Ch & Chyd Mfche (1981). Methodist & Wesleyan Methodist Mfche (1981)

LEICESTERSHIRE

Leicestershire Monumental Inscriptions by P. Moll (1975) TS, 3 vols. All legible inscriptions in 165 churchyards, in general to 1900 only

The Incised Slabs of Leicestershire & Rutland by F. A. Greenhill (1958) 25-190. Every church now or formerly containing incised slabs

ABKETTLEBY Chyd TS (c. 1954)

APPLEBY Ch *Top* 2 (1790) 71-73

ARNESBY Chyd TS (1946-47)

ASHBY MAGNA Chyd TS (1947)

AYLESTONE Chyd TS (1946-47)

BARKESTONE Ch & Chyd TS (1974)

BARTON IN THE BEANS Baptist B.g. TS (1946-47)

BARWELL Chyd TS (1946-47)

BEEBY Chyd TS (c. 1912)

BELGRAVE Chyd TS (c. 1912); TS (1946-47)

BELTON Chyd extr TS (1946-47)

BIRSTALL Chyd TS (1946-47); extr TS (1940)

BRAUNSTONE Chyd TS (1946-47)

BREEDON ON THE HILL Ch & Chyd (1982)

BURROUGH ON THE HILL Chyd TS (c. 1912)

BURTON OVERY Chyd TS (c. 1912); TS (c. 1912); TS (1946-47)

CADEBY Chyd TS (1946-47)

CARLTON CURLIEU Ch & Chyd TS (c. 1912)

CLAYBROOK Chyd TS (1946-47) copied from *The History & Antiquities of Claybrook* by A. Macaulay (1791)

COLD OVERTON Ch TS (c. 1912)

COSSINGTON Ch & Chyd extr TS (c. 1940)

COTESBACH Ch & Chyd TS (c. 1912)

CRANOE Chyd TS (1946-47)

GALBY Ch TS (c. 1912)

GILMORTON Chyd TS (c. 1912)

GLOOSTON Chyd TS (1946-47)

HIGHAM ON THE HILL Ch extr TS of parish register (1932)

HUGGLESCOTE Chyd TS (1949-47). Baptist B.g. TS (1946-47)

HUMBERSTONE Ch *Humberstone: A Brief History of the Church and the Manors* by G. E. Kendall (1916) 24-27

KING'S NORTON Ch TS (c. 1912) from J. Nichols' *History of Leicestershire* (1795, 2nd edn 1815)

KIRBY BELLARS Chyd TS (c. 1912)

KIRBY MUXLOE Ch & Chyd TS of parish register (1966)

KNIPTON Chyd TS (1979)

LEICESTER All Saints Ch & Chyd TS (c. 1912); Chyd TS (1947). St Leonard Ch TS (1986); Chyd TS (1946-47). St Margaret Ch & Chyd MS (1912); Chyd TS (1946-47). St

Martin Ch MS (1939); Chyd TS (1947). St Mary de Castro Chyd TS (1912); TS (1948). St Nicholas Chyd TS (c. 1912); extr TS (1946-47). Bond Street Congregational B.g. TS (1946-47). Great Meeting *The Epitaphs in the Graveyard & Chapel of the Great Meeting, Leicester* by A. H. Paget (1912). Harvey Lane Baptist B.g. TS (1946-47); TS (1950)

LOCKINGTON Chyd TS (c. 1912)

LOUGHBOROUGH General Cmy TS (c. 1955)

LUTTERWORTH Ch *Lutterworth* by A. H. Dyson (1913) 118-122

MARKET HARBOROUGH St Mary in Arden Ch & Chyd TS (1983)

MEASHAM Baptist B.g. TS (1986)

MELTON MOWBRAY Ch & Chyd extr *Melton Mowbray in Olden Times* by J. Ward (1879) 173-177. Central Methodist Chap and B.g. TS (1972)

MOUNTSORREL Baptist B.g. TS of parish register of Knipton (1939)

NEWTON LINFORD Ch & Chyd TS (1970). Chyd extr TS of parish register (1938)

OADBY Chyd TS (1946-47)

OSGATHORPE Cmy TS (1986)

QUORN General Baptist Chap & B.g. extr TS (1946-47)

RATBY Chyd TS (1946-47)

ROTHLEY Baptist B.g. extr TS (1946-47)

SAPCOTE Ch & Chyd (Spencer family) *Frag Gen* 7 (1902) 147-148

SCRAPTOFT Ch & Chyd TS (1946-47)

STONTON WYVILLE Chyd TS (1946-47)

STRETTON EN LE FIELD Ch & Chyd TS (1986)

STRETTON, GREAT Chyd TS (c. 1912)

STRETTON, LITTLE Chyd TS (c. 1912)

SWITHLAND Chyd TS (1946-47); extr TS (1943)

THURCASTON Ch & Chyd TS (1946-47)

THURLASTON Ch *The History of Thurlaston* by J. O. Hulme (1904) 121 123 129-141

THURMASTON Ch & Chyd TS (1946-47)

WANLIP Ch & Chyd TS of parish register (1932). Chyd TS (c. 1912)

WISTOW Chyd TS (c. 1912)

WOODHOUSE EAVES Baptist B.g. TS (1946-47)

WYMESWOLD Old Baptist B.g. TS (1973). See also NOTTINGHAMSHIRE

LINCOLNSHIRE

Lincolnshire Church Notes made by Gervase Holles 1634-42 ed by R. E. G. Cole (1911).

Lincoln Record Soc. vol. 1. Monuments from churches throughout the county

Lincolnshire Church Notes made by William John Monson 1828-1840 ed by John 9th Lord Monson (1936). Lincoln Record Soc. vol. 31. Monuments from churches throughout the county

"Monumental Inscriptions from other counties relating to Lincolnshire" in *Lincolnshire Notes & Queries* 1 (1889) 228-230; 2 (1891) 49-51 68-70 239-240

ALVINGHAM Ch & Chyd TS (1981)

ANCASTER Chyd TS (1980)

ANWICK Ch & Chyd TS (1984)

APLEY Old Chyd TS (1980)

ASGARBY (by SLEAFORD) Ch & Chyd TS (1984)

ASGARBY (by SPILSBY) Ch & Chyd TS (1983)

ASHBY CUM FENBY Ch & Chyd TS (1985) copied c. 1890; TS (1984)

ASHBY, WEST Ch & Chyd TS (1983)

ASLACKBY Ch MS of parish register (1961)

ASTERBY Ch & Chyd TS (1983)

ASWARBY Ch & Chyd TS (1983)

AUBOURN Ch & Chyd *Monumental Inscriptions, Deanery of Graffoe 2 – Aubourn* by R. E. G. Cole (1898); index TS (1983)

AUNSBY Chyd TS (1980)

AYLESBY Ch & Chyd xerox of MS (1983)

BARKWITH, WEST Chyd TS (1984)

BARNOLDBY-LE-BECK Ch & Chyd TS (1984)

BARROW Ch *Lincs Notes & Queries* 10 (1909) 146-150

BARROWBY *Notts FHS RS* 20 (1982)

BARTON St Mary Ch *Lincs Notes & Queries* 10 (1909) 186-189. St Peter Ch *ibid* 180-186

BASSINGTHORPE Ch & Chyd TS (1979)

BAUMBER Chyd TS (1977)

BEELSBY Ch TS (1983)

BEESBY Chyd TS (1984)

BIGBY Ch & Chyd TS (1984)

BINBROOK Ch & Chyd TS (1984). Old Chyd TS (1985)

BISCATHORPE Ch & Chyd TS (1980)

BITCHFIELD Ch & Chyd TS (1979)

BLYBURGH Ch & extr Chyd *History of Blyburgh* by Oxoniensis (1902)

BOOTHBY GRAFFOE Chyd TS (1982)

BOOTHBY PAGNELL Chyd list TS (1980)

BOSTON Holy Trinity Ch & Chyd TS (1983). St Botolph Ch *The History & Antiquities of Boston* by Pishey Thompson (1856) 192-198. St John Chyd list TS (1983)

BOULTHAM Ch & Chyd list TS (1981)

BRACEBRIDGE Ch & Chyd TS (1982)
BRACEBY Chyd TS (1980)
BRADLEY Ch & Chyd TS (1983)
BRAUNCEWELL Ch & Chyd TS (1970)
BRIGSLEY St Peter Ch & Chyd TS (1985)
 copied c. 1890. St Helen Ch & Chyd TS (1982)
BURGH LE MARSH Ch & Chyd TS (1985).
 Chyd *YOM* misc vol. Baptist B.g. TS (1985)
BURTON COGGLES Ch & Chyd TS (1984)
BURWELL Ch & Chyd TS (1982)
BUSLINGTHORPE Ch & Chyd TS (1984)
CABOURN Ch & Chyd TS (1984)
CAENBY Chyd TS (1983)
CAISTOR Ch *Gent Mag* (1829) II, 223; Ch &
 Chyd TS (1984). Dissenters B.g. TS (1984).
 See also CLIXBY
CARLBY Ch *Gent Mag* (1864) II, 502-503
CARLTON LE MOORLAND Ch *Lincs Notes
 & Queries* 7 (1902) 148-149
CARLTON, LITTLE Chyd TS (1982)
CHERRY WILLINGHAM Ch & Chyd TS
 (1979)
CLAXBY Ch & Chyd TS (1984)
CLEE, NEW Ch TS (1983)
CLEE, OLD Ch & Chyd TS (1983). Chyd *YOM*
 misc vol; TS (n.d.)
CLEETHORPES Chyd TS (1985) copied 1891.
 Cmy, Trinity Road TS (1986)
CLIXBY Ch & Chyd TS (1982)
COATES, GREAT Ch & Chyd TS (1982);
 Chyd *YOM* misc vol
COATES, LITTLE Chyd *YOM* misc vol; TS
 (1983)
COCKERINGTON Chyd TS (1975)
COCKERINGTON, NORTH see
 ALVINGHAM
COLSTERWORTH Chyd TS (1981)
CORBY GLEN Ch & Chyd TS (1985)
COVENHAM St Bartholomew Chyd TS (1981).
 St Mary Chyd TS (1981)
CREETON Ch & Chyd TS (1984)
CROFT Chyd *YOM* misc vol
CROWLE Ch & Chyd TS (1985). Baptist B.g.
 TS (1984)
CROXBY Ch & Chyd TS (1984)
CUXWOLD Ch & Chyd TS (1984)
DALBY Ch & Chyd TS (1984)
DEMBLEBY Old Ch & Chyd TS (1980) taken
 1834; Ch & Chyd TS (1980)
DENTON Ch & Chyd TS (1986)
DODDINGTON-PIGOT Ch & Chyd
 *Monumental Inscriptions, Deanery of Graffoe
 1 -Doddington* by R. E. G. Cole (1898); extr
 The Registers of Doddington-Pigot by R. E.
 G. Cole (1898) 93
EDENHAM Ch (Bertie family) *Gent Mag*
 (1808) I, 19-22; Ch *Gent Mag* (1864) II,

763-769
ELKINGTON Ch TS (1982)
EVEDON Ch & Chyd TS (1984)
EWERBY Ch & Chyd TS (1984)
FARFORTH CUM MAIDENWELL Ch &
 Chyd TS (1980)
FLETE Ch *Gent Mag* (1798) II, 1094
FOTHERBY Ch & Chyd TS (1984); Chyd
 YOM misc vol
FRIESTHORPE Ch & Chyd TS (1985)
FRIESTON Ch & Chyd TS (1984)
FRITHVILLE Chyd TS (1983)
GAINSBOROUGH index TS (1931)
GAYTON LE WOLD Chyd TS (1982)
GLENTWORTH Ch & Chyd MS & TS (1979)
GOLTHO Chyd TS (1983)
GONERBY, GREAT Chyd TS (1980)
GRAINSBY Ch & Chyd TS (1984)
GRANTHAM Ch Hearne IV, 196-198. Brook
 Street Cmy TS (1979)
GRASBY Ch & Chyd TS (1984)
GRIMSBY, GREAT Ch *The Register Book of
 the Parish Church of St. James, Great
 Grimsby 1538-1812* by G. S. Stephenson
 (1884) 14-16; Chyd *YOM* misc vol. Doughty
 Road Cmy TS (1985)
GRIMSBY, LITTLE Ch & Chyd TS (1981)
HABROUGH Ch & Chyd TS (1983)
HACEBY Chyd TS (1980)
HALTHAM ON BAIN Chyd TS (1980)
HAMERINGHAM Ch & Chyd TS (1983)
HANNAH CUM HAGNABY Chyd TS (1983)
HAREBY Ch & Chyd TS (1983)
HARPSWELL Ch & Chyd TS (1984)
HARRINGTON Ch *Top* 4 (1791) 179-182
HATCLIFFE Ch & Chyd TS (1983)
HATTON Chyd TS (1984)
HAUGH Ch TS (1981)
HAUGHAM Ch & Chyd TS (1981)
HAWERBY CUM BEESBY Ch & Chyd TS
 (1983)
HEALING Ch TS (1985) copied c. 1890. Ch &
 Chyd MS & TS (1983)
HEAPHAM Chyd TS (1981)
HECKINGTON Ch *Notes on St Andrews
 Church Heckington* by H.T.S. (1912) 8-20.
 Chyd TS (1985)
HECKINGTON, EAST Chyd TS (1984)
HEMSWELL Ch, Old Chyd & New Cmy TS
 (1984)
HEYDOUR Ch *The Register of Haydor 1559-
 1649* by Canon G. P. Deedes (1897) 60-62.
 Chyd TS (1976)
HOLBEACH Chyd TS (1980)
HOLTON LE CLAY Ch, Chyd & Cmy TS
 (1983)
HORBLING Ch *Registers of the Parish of*

Horbling by H. Peet (1895) xxi-xxv
HORNCASTLE Ch & Chyd TS (1980)
HORSINGTON Ch & Chyd TS (1981)
HOWELL Chyd TS (1984)
HUMBERSTONE Ch & Chyd TS (1983). Cmy TS (1983)
HYKEHAM, NORTH Chyd TS (1979)
IMMINGHAM Cmy TS (1985)
INGOLDSBY Chyd TS (1979)
IRBY UPON HUMBER Ch & Chyd TS (1983)
KEDDINGTON Chyd TS (1979)
KEELBY Ch & Chyd TS (1984). Chyd TS (1985) copied c. 1890
KELBY Chyd TS (1980)
KELSTERN Ch & Chyd TS (1984)
KETTLETHORPE Ch & Chyd TS (1985)
KINGERBY Ch & Chyd TS (1981)
KIRKBY CUM OSGODBY Ch & Chyd TS (1981). Chyd MS (1981)
KIRKBY LAYTHORPE Ch & Chyd TS (1984)
KIRKBY ON BAIN Chyd TS (1980)
KIRKBY UNDERWOOD Chyd TS (1979)
KIRKSTEAD Ch & Chyd TS (1984)
KIRMOND LE MIRE Ch & Chyd TS (1983)
KYME Chyd list of surnames MS (n.d.)
LACEBY Chyd TS (1985) copied c. 1890; TS (1981). Cmy TS (1984)
LANGTON BY HORNCASTLE Chyd TS (1983)
LANGTON BY PARTNEY Ch & Chyd TS (1984)
LANGTON BY WRAGBY Ch & Chyd TS (1985)
LEASINGHAM Ch & Chyd TS (1979); Chyd MS (1979)
LEGSBY Chyd TS (1980)
LENTON Chyd TS (1980)
LINCOLN Cathedral Bloom's Yorkshire MSS vol 7, 226-230 (copied 1892). St Margaret Ch TS (1985). St Mark Chyd TS (1978). St Martin Ch *Lincs Notes & Queries* 12 (1912) 17-19; B.g., Garmston Street TS (1981). St Michael Ch & Chyd TS (1985). St Paul in the Bail Chyd TS (1978). St Peter in Eastgate Ch & Chyd TS (1985). St Swithin Ch & Chyd TS (1985).
LISSINGTON Chyd TS (n.d.)
LONDONTHORPE Chyd TS (1979)
LOUTH Ch *Top* 4 (1791) 161-165; *Lincs Notes & Queries* 12 (1912) 21-26. Ch & Chyd TS (1980)
LUDBOROUGH Ch & Chyd TS (1984)
LUDDINGTON Chyd TS (1985)
LUSBY Ch & Chyd TS (1983)
LYNWODE Chyd TS (n.d.)
MANTON Old Ch & Chyd *Gent Mag* (1864) II, 367-368

MAREHAM ON THE HILL Ch & Chyd TS (1983)
MARKET STAINTON Ch & Chyd TS (1984)
MARKET RASEN See RASEN, MARKET
MARSHCHAPEL Ch & Chyd TS (n.d.)
MARTIN BY HORNCASTLE Ch & Chyd TS (1979)
METHERINGHAM Ch & Chyd TS (1982)
MIDDLE RASEN See RASEN, DRAX and RASEN, TUPHOLME
MININGSBY Chyd TS (1983)
MOORBY Chyd TS (1982)
MUCKTON Chyd TS (1981)
NETTLETON Ch & Chyd TS (1984)
NEWTON Chyd TS (1981)
NORTHORPE Ch & Chyd TS (1981)
ORMSBY, NORTH Chyd TS (1981)
OSBOURNBY Ch & Chyd TS (1974)
OXCOMBE Ch & Chyd TS (1981)
PANTON Ch & Chyd TS (1980)
PICKWORTH Ch & Chyd TS (1981)
PONTON, GREAT Chyd TS (1980)
PONTON, LITTLE Chyd TS (1980)
RAITHBY CUM MALTBY Ch & Chyd TS (1982)
RANBY Chyd TS (1984)
RAND Ch MS (n.d.). Ch & Chyd TS (1984)
RASEN, DRAX Chyd TS (1982)
RASEN, MARKET Ch & Chyd TS (1982)
RASEN, TUPHOLME Ch & Chyd TS (1982)
RAUCEBY Ch & Chyd TS (1985)
RAVENDALE, EAST Ch & Chyd TS (1984)
REEPHAM Ch & Chyd TS (1985)
RESTON, NORTH Chyd TS (1982)
RESTON, SOUTH Chyd TS (1981)
RIBY Ch & Chyd TS (1983). Chyd TS (1985) copied c. 1890
RIGSBY Ch & Chyd TS (1984)
ROTHWELL Ch & Chyd TS (1984)
ROUGHTON Ch & Chyd TS (1980)
RUCKLAND Ch & Chyd TS (1981)
RUSKINGTON Chyd TS (1981)
SALTFLEETBY ST CLEMENT Ch & Chyd TS (1984)
SALTFLEETBY ST PETER Chyd TS (1984)
SAPPERTON Chyd TS (1980)
SCARTHO Ch & Chyd TS (1982)
SCOTTON Ch & Chyd TS (1982)
SCOTT WILLOUGHBY Chyd TS (1981)
SCREDINGTON Ch & Chyd TS (c. 1982)
SCRIVELSBY Ch & Chyd TS (1979)
SEARBY Ch & Chyd TS (1984)
SIBSEY Chyd TS (1981)
SKENDLEBY Ch & Chyd TS (1984)
SKIDBROOK Chyd TS (1983)
SKILLINGTON Chyd xerox of MS (1977)
SNARFORD Ch & Chyd TS (1984)

SNELLAND Chyd TS (1984)
SOMERBY Ch & Chyd TS (1984)
SOMERBY, OLD Chyd TS (1983)
SOMERCOTES, SOUTH Chyd TS (1983)
SOTBY Chyd TS (1981)
SOUTHREY Ch & Chyd TS (1984)
SPANBY Chyd TS (1982)
SPILSBY Ch extr *A History of Spilsby* by H.
 C. Smith (1892) 49-85
SPRINGTHORPE Chyd TS (1981)
STAINFIELD Ch & Chyd TS (1984)
STAINTON BY LANGWORTH Ch & Chyd
 TS (1984)
STAINTON LE VALE Chyd TS (1983)
STALLINGBOROUGH Ch & Chyd TS (1983)
STAMFORD St John Ch *The Monumental
 Tablets in St. John's Church* by Thomas
 Sandell (n.d.); Chyd *The Gravestones of St.
 John's Churchyard, Stamford* by Thomas
 Sandell (n.d.). St Michael Ch & Chyd TS
 (1974)
STEWTON Chyd TS (1982)
STIXWOULD Ch & Chyd TS (1981)
STOW Ch *Gent Mag* (1831) I, 493-495
STROXTON Chyd TS (1980)
SUTTERBY Chyd TS (1980)
SUTTON ON SEA Chyd TS (1972)
SWALLOW Ch & Chyd TS (1984)
SWARBY Chyd TS (1980)
SWAYFIELD Ch & Chyd TS (1984)
SWINHOPE Ch, Chyd & Cmy TS (1983)
SWINSTEAD Ch & Chyd TS (1984)
TATTERSHALL Ch & Chyd TS (1982)
TEMPLE BRUER Chyd TS (1982)
TETNEY Ch, Chyd & Cmy TS (1983)
THIMBLEBY Ch & Chyd TS (1981)
THORESBY, SOUTH Ch & Chyd TS (1984)
THORESWAY Chyd TS (1983)
THORGANBY Ch & Chyd TS (1983)
THORNTON BY HORNCASTLE Ch & Chyd
 TS (1980)
THORPE ST PETER Chyd TS (n.d.)
THRECKINGHAM Ch & Chyd TS (1981)
THURLBY Ch *Lincs Notes & Queries* 12 (1912)
 19-21
TOTHILL Chyd TS (1983)
TOYNTON, HIGH Chyd TS (1982)
ULCEBY Ch & Chyd TS (1984)
UTTERBY Ch & Chyd TS (1984)
WADDINGHAM Ch & Chyd TS (1984)
WADDINGTON Ch & Chyd TS (1980)
WADDINGWORTH Chyd TS (1983)
WAITHE Ch & Chyd TS (1983). Chyd TS
 (n.d.)
WALESBY All Saints Ch & Chyd TS (1985). St
 Mary Ch & Chyd TS (1985)
WALCOT Chyd TS (1980)

WALMSGATE Chyd TS (1982)
WALTHAM Ch & Chyd TS (1982); Chyd TS
 (1985) copied 1891. Ings Lane Cmy TS (1983)
WELL Ch & Chyd TS (1983)
WELLINGORE Chyd TS (1984)
WELTON LE WOLD Chyd TS (1982)
WHAPLODE Ch *The Parish Church of St
 Mary, Whaplode* by W. E. Foster (1889) 48-50
WICKENBY Ch & Chyd TS (1984)
WILKSBY Ch & Chyd TS (1984)
WILSFORD Chyd TS (1979)
WISPINGTON Ch MS (n.d.). Chyd TS (1983)
WITHCALL Ch & Chyd TS (1982)
WITHERN Ch & Chyd TS (1984)
WOLD NEWTON Ch & Chyd TS (1984)
WOOD ENDERBY Chyd TS (1981)
WOODHALL, OLD Chyd TS (1983)
WOODHALL SPA Chyd TS (1983);
 corrections TS (1984)
WYHAM Ch & Chyd TS (1981)
YARBURGH Chyd TS (1981)

NORTHUMBERLAND

Northumberland M.I. (n.d.) MS. Tynemouth —
 Christ Church, Abbey, and Priory; North
 Shields, Old Cmy; Wallsend, Holy Cross;
 Earsdon Chyd; Preston Cmy

Northumbrian Monuments (Newcastle upon
 Tyne Record Series 4 (1924)). Miscellaneous
 inscriptions associated with shields of arms
 and effigies prior to 1666

ALLENDALE Chyd TS (1975)
ALNHAM Ch & Chyd MS (1973)
ALWINTON see HOLYSTONE
BEDLINGTON Ch & Chyd TS (1977)
BELTINGHAM Chyd TS (1975)
BENWELL Tower Chapel B.g. MS (n.d.)
BLANCHLAND Chyd *Proceedings of Society
 of Antiquaries of Newcastle on Tyne* 5 ser, 1:3
 (Summer 1952) 111-117
BLYTH Old Chapel TS (1975) from MS at
 Newcastle Central Reference Library
BOLAM Chyd TS (1974)
BOLTON Ch & Chyd MS (c. 1972)
BOTHAL Chyd TS (1975)
BRANXTON Chyd TS (1982)
BROOMHAUGH Baptist B.g. TS (1974)
BYWELL St Andrew Chyd *Misc Gen et Her*
 4 ser ii (1908) 88-89; TS (1974). St Peter Chyd
 *Proceedings of Society of Antiquaries of
 Newcastle on Tyne* 5 ser, 1:3 (Summer 1952)
 107-111; TS (1974)

12

CARHAM see MINDRUM
CHATTON Chyd TS (1974)
CHILLINGHAM Chyd TS (1974)
CHOLLERTON Chyd TS (1975)
CORBRIDGE Chyd TS (1975)
CORNHILL Ch & Chyd TS (1982)
DALTON see NEWBURN
DINNINGTON Ch & Chyd TS (1986)
EARSDON Ch & Chyd TS (1976)
EDLINGHAM Ch & Chyd MS (1972). See also
  BOLTON
FORD Chyd TS (1978)
HALTON Chyd TS (1974)
HALTWHISTLE Chyd TS (1976). See also
  BELTINGHAM
HARTBURN Ch & Chyd MS (1971)
HEBRON Chyd TS (1975)
HEDDON ON THE WALL Chyd TS (1974)
HEXHAM Abbey Ch & Chyd TS (1975)
  (includes earlier copies). Cmy TS (1975). St.
  Mary's R.C. Chyd TS (1975)
HOLYSTONE Ch & Chyd TS (1975)
HORTON Chyd TS (1976)
INGRAM Chyd TS (1974)
KIRKHARLE Ch & Chyd TS (c. 1974); Chyd
  TS (1975)
KIRKHAUGH Chyd TS (c. 1975) from
  transcript at Newcastle Reference Library
KIRKHEATON Chyd TS (1975)
KIRKNEWTON Ch & Chyd extr *Archaeologia
  Aeliana* 3 ser, 21 (1924) 155-161
KYLOE Chyd TS (1974)
LAMBLEY Chyd TS (1975) from MS (1911) at
  Newcastle Central Reference Library
LONGHORSLEY Ch & Chyd MS (1972)
MELDON Ch & Chyd MS (1971)
MINDRUM Chyd TS (1974)
MITFORD Chyd TS (1974)
MORPETH Ch & Chyd TS (1976)
NETHERWITTON Ch & Chyd MS (1971)
NEWBIGGIN (WOODHORN) Ch & Chyd TS
  (1978)
NEWBURN Chyd & Dalton Chapel TS (1975)
NEWCASTLE UPON TYNE All Saints Ch &
  Chyd *A Historical and Descriptive Account of
  All Saints' Church in Newcastle upon Tyne* by
  T. Sopwith (1826) 29-40 101-106; *A
  Descriptive and Historical Account of the
  Town and County of Newcastle upon Tyne* by
  E. Mackenzie, vol. 1 (1827) 298-300 312 315.
  St Andrew Ch & Chyd *A Collection of
  Armorial Bearings, Inscriptions, etc. in the
  Parochial Chapel of Saint Andrew, Newcastle
  upon Tyne* by M. A. Richardson (1818);
  Mackenzie, *op. cit.* 329-334. St Ann TS (1975).
  St John Ch & Chyd Mackenzie, *op. cit.* 347-
  353; *The Church of St John the Baptist,*

Newcastle on Tyne by J. W. Fawcett (1909)
  11-19 27-28; Index TS (1906); see also
  BENWELL. St Nicholas Ch & Chyd
  Mackenzie, *op. cit.* 256-275; *A Descriptive and
  Historical Account of the Monuments &
  Tombstones in the Church of St Nicholas,
  Newcastle upon Tyne* by R. Welford (1880);
  Chyd TS (1905). Ballast Hills B.g. extr
  Mackenzie, *op. cit.* 409-413. Percy Street B.g.
  extr Mackenzie, *op. cit.* 414
NORTH SHIELDS Chyd TS (c. 1951). Index
  TS (1980)
OVINGHAM Ch & Chyd MS (1913) (bound
  with parish register); MS (n.d.); Chyd extr
  Misc Gen et Her 4 ser i (1906) 225
PONTELAND Ch & Chyd TS (1986)
PRESTON Chyd MS (n.d.)
ST JOHN LEE Chyd TS (1975)
SHOTLEY St Andrew Chyd TS (1974). St John
  Chyd TS (1974)
STAMFORDHAM Chyd TS (1974)
STANNINGTON Chyd TS (1975)
THOCKRINGTON Chyd TS (1975)
TYNEMOUTH see NORTH SHIELDS
ULGHAM Ch & Chyd MS (1972)
WARKWORTH Ch & Chyd *Epitaphs and
  Monumental Inscriptions of Warkworth
  Church and Churchyard* by M. H. Dand and
  J. C. Hodgson (1890)
WHALTON Chyd TS (1974)
WHITTONSTALL Chyd TS (1974)
WIDDRINGTON Chyd MS (1972)
WOODHORN Ch & Chyd TS (1978)

NOTTINGHAMSHIRE

*Notes on the Churches of Nottinghamshire.
  Hundred of Bingham* by J. T. Godfrey
  (1907). Extracts from many churches
  throughout the hundred

ANNESLEY Chyd TS (1947)
ARNOLD Chyd extr *A History of Arnold,
  Nottinghamshire* by R. W. King & J. Russell
  (1913) 69-72. Ch & Chyd *Notts FHS RS* 44
  (1985)
ASKHAM *Notts FHS RS* 44 (1985)
BARNBY IN THE WILLOWS *Notts FHS RS*
  51 (1986)
BARTON-IN-FABIS *Notts FHS RS* 2 (1979)
BASFORD Ch & Chyd MS of parish registers
  1538-1719 compiled by L. B. & H. Lander
  (1939). New Cmy *ibid.*
BESTWOOD *Notts FHS RS* 18 (1982)
BILBOROUGH Ch & Chyd *Notts FHS RS* 20
  (1982)

13

BLEASBY *Notts FHS* 20 (1982)
BLYTH *Notts FHS RS* 18 (1982)
BOLE *Notts FHS RS* 44 (1985)
BRAMCOTE *Notts FHS RS* 51 (1986)
BRIDGFORD, EAST Ch *East Bridgford, Nottinghamshire; the Story of an English Village* by Rev A. Du Boulay Hill (1932) 129-137. Ch & Chyd *Notts FHS RS* 12 (1981)
BRIDGFORD, WEST Chyd *Misc Gen et Her* NS2 (1877) 341-344
BRINSLEY Chyd TS (1947)
BULCOTE Chyd TS (1975). *Notts FHS RS* 18 (1982)
BURTON JOYCE Ch *Thoroton Society Transactions* 2-3 (1898) 34-39. *Notts FHS RS* 18 (1982)
CALVERTON *Notts FHS RS* 20 (1982)
CARBURTON Ch MS of parish register (1888) 34-36
CAR COLSTON *Notts FHS RS* 20 (1982)
CARRINGTON *Notts FHS RS* 44 (1985)
CAUNTON Chyd MS (1980). *Notts FHS RS* 34 (1984)
CLARBOROUGH *Notts FHS RS* 51 (1986)
CLIFTON Chyd TS (1947). *Notts FHS RS* 2 (1979)
CLIFTON, NORTH *Notts FHS RS* 12 (1981)
CLIFTON, SOUTH *Notts FHS RS* 12 (1981)
COLLINGHAM Baptist Chap & B.g. TS (1985); *Notts FHS RS* 44 (1975)
COLSTON BASSETT Ch & Chyd MS of parish register 2 (1924) 195-224. Chyd *Thoroton Society Record Series* 9 (1942) 59-64. *Notts FHS RS* 6 (1979)
COLWICK *Notts FHS RS* 20 (1982)
COSSALL *Notts FHS RS* 51 (1986)
COTGRAVE *Notts FHS RS* 44 (1985)
COTHAM *Notts FHS RS* 51 (1986)
COTTAM *Notts FHS RS* 44 (1985)
CROMWELL *Notts FHS RS* 18 (1982)
CROPWELL BISHOP *Notts FHS RS* 2 (1979)
DENBY Chyd MS (n.d.)
DUNHAM-ON-TRENT Ch extr *History of Dunham-on-Trent* by Rev Howard Chadwick (1924) 86. *Notts FHS RS* 44 (1985)
EASTWOOD Chyd TS (1947)
EDWALTON Chyd *Misc Gen et Her* NS2 (1877) 307-308. *Notts FHS RS* 6 (1979)
EDWINSTOWE Ch & Chyd *Edwinstowe Registers* by G. W. Marshall (1891) 165-186
ELSTON *Notts FHS RS* 39 (1985)
FARNDON *Notts FHS RS* 51 (1986)
FLAWFORD Chyd *Notts & Derbyshire N & Q* 2 (1894) 134-135
FLEDBOROUGH Chyd TS (1968)
GEDLING *Notts FHS RS* 21 (1982)
GONALSTON *Notts FHS RS* 21 (1982)

GRANBY Chyd TS (1973). *Notts FHS RS* 1 (1979)
GREASELEY Ch & Chyd *Griseleia: History of Greaseley* by R. Baron Von Hube (1901) 133-144 148-151. Chyd TS (1947)
HALLOUGHTON *Notts FHS RS* 21 (1982)
HAYTON *Notts FHS RS* 51 (1986)
HEADON Ch *Headon Registers* by Edith Hobday (1902) 149; *Notts FHS RS* 44 (1985)
HICKLING *Notts FHS RS* 1 (1979)
HOCKERTON *Notts FHS RS* 54 (1986)
HOLME PIERREPOINT *Notts FHS RS* 21 (1982)
HOVERINGHAM Ch & Chyd *Notts FHS RS* 34 (1984)
HUCKNALL TORKARD Chyd extr *Notts FHS Journal* 2:10 (1978) 14-17 (from *History of Hucknall Torkard* by J. H. Beardmore, 1909). Chyd TS (1947)
KELHAM Ch & Chyd *Notts FHS RS* 54 (1986)
KEYWORTH *Notts FHS RS* 12 (1981)
KILVINGTON Ch *Notts FHS RS* 54 (1986)
KIMBERLEY Ch & Chyd *Notts FHS RS* 54 (1986)
KINGSTON ON SOAR Ch & Chyd *Notts FHS RS* 54 (1986)
KINOULTON Chyd & Old Cmy TS (1971). *Notts FHS RS* 44 (1985)
KIRBY WOODHOUSE Baptist Chap *Notts FHS RS* 47 (1985)
KIRKBY-IN-ASHFIELD Ch & extr Chyd *Gen* NS23 (1907) 252-257
KIRKLINGTON Ch & Chyd *Notts FHS RS* 54 (1986)
KNEETON *Notts FHS RS* 12 (1981)
LAMBLEY Ch, Chyd & B.g. *Notts FHS RS* 54 (1986)
LANEHAM *Notts FHS RS* 47 (1985)
LANGAR *Notts FHS RS* 47 (1985)
LAXTON Ch & Chyd TS (n.d.)
LEAKE, EAST *Notts FHS RS* 13 (1981). Baptist B.g. *ibid*
LEAKE, WEST *Notts FHS RS* 13 (1981)
LENTON *Notts FHS RS* 27 (1983). Priory Church *Notts FHS RS* 47 (1985)
LINBY Chyd TS (1947)
LITTLEBOROUGH *Notts FHS RS* 47 (1985)
LOWDHAM *Notts FHS RS* 18 (1982)
MANSFIELD Ch & Chyd xerox from *Historic Mansfield* 1 by A. S. Buxton (c. 1800, repr 1972)
MAPLEBECK Ch & Chyd *Notts FHS RS* 54 (1986)
MISTERTON *Notts FHS RS* 47 (1985)
MORTON *Notts FHS RS* 34 (1984)
MUSKHAM, NORTH *Notts FHS RS* 12 (1981)

MUSKHAM, SOUTH *Notts FHS RS* 13 (1981)
NEWTHORPE Baptist B.g. TS (1947); *Notts FHS RS* 47 (1985)
NOTTINGHAM St Mary the Virgin Ch *Thoroton Society Transactions* 21 (1917) 48-55; Bellar Gate Cholera B.g. *Notts FHS RS* 54 (1986). Mount Street B.g. *Monumental Inscriptions in the Baptist Burial Ground, Mount Street, Nottingham* by James Ward (1899). Friar Lane B.g. *The History of Friar Lane Baptist Church, Nottingham* by J. T. Godfrey & J. Ward (1903) 89-127. General Cmy extr MS (1911)
NUTHALL *Notts FHS RS* 19 (1982)
ORSTON *Notts FHS RS* 12 (1981)
OXTON *Notts FHS RS* 39 (1985)
PAPPLEWICK Ch & Chyd *Notts FHS RS* 34 (1984)
PLUMTREE *Notts FHS RS* 12 (1981)
RADFORD, NEW Chyd TS (1947)
RADFORD, OLD *Notts FHS RS* 39 (1985)
RAMPTON *Notts FHS RS* 47 (1985)
RATCLIFFE ON SOAR Ch & Chyd *Notts FHS RS* 54 (1986)
REDMILE *Notts FHS RS* 1 (1979)
REMPSTONE *Notts FHS RS* 13 (1981). St Peter in the Rushes Old Chyd *ibid*
SANDIACRE *Notts FHS RS* 13 (1981)
SCARLE, SOUTH Ch & Chyd *Notts FHS RS* 19 (1982)
SCARRINGTON *Notts FHS RS* 6 (1979)
SCREVETON Ch *Gen* 7 (1883) 199-204
SELSTON Chyd TS (1947). Congregational B.g. MS (n.d.)
SHELFORD Ch & Chyd *Notts FHS RS* 34 (1984)
SHELTON Ch & Chyd *The Parish Registers of Shelton* by T. M. Blagg (1900) 59-63. *Notts FHS RS* 34 (1984)
SOUTHWELL Baptist B.g. TS (1962)
STANFORD-ON-SOAR Ch *Top & Gen* 2 (1790) 242-245. Chyd TS (1973)
STANTON-ON-THE-WOLD Chyd TS (1947)
STAPLEFORD Ch & Chyd TS (1976). *Notts FHS RS* 19 (1982)
STOKE, EAST Ch & Chyd *Notts FHS RS* 39 (1985)
STOKEHAM *Notts FHS RS* 47 (1985)
STRELLEY Chyd TS (1947). *Notts FHS RS* 19 (1982)
SUTTON BONNINGTON St Anne Chyd *Notts FHS RS* 54 (1986). St Michael Chyd *ibid*. Marlpit Hill Cmy *ibid*
SUTTON-IN-ASHFIELD Chyd TS (1946)
SYERSTON *Notts FHS RS* 39 (1985)
TEVERSAL Ch & extr Chyd *Gent Mag* (1810) I, 120-122

THORPE Ch & Chyd *Notts FHS RS* 47 (1985)
TOLLERTON *Notts FHS RS* 19 (1982)
TRESWELL *Notts FHS RS* 47 (1985)
TROWELL Ch & Chyd *Notts FHS RS* 54 (1986). Chyd TS (1947)
TYTHBY *Notts FHS RS* 54 (1986)
UPTON *Notts FHS RS* 39 (1985)
WHATTON-IN-THE-VALE *Notts FHS RS* 15 (1981)
WILFORD Ch & extr Chyd *Misc Gen et Her* NS3 (1880) 163-164 172-176. *Notts FHS RS* 15 (1981)
WILLOUGHBY-ON-THE-WOLDS *Notts FHS RS* 15 (1981)
WINKBOURNE Ch *Monumental Inscriptions [of Derbyshire]* by White Watson (1806) MS
WOODBOROUGH *Notts FHS RS* 21 (1982)
WYMESWOLD *Notts FHS RS* 15 (1981). See also LEICESTERSHIRE
WYSALL *Notts FHS RS* 19 (1982)

RUTLAND

Blore's History of Rutland (1811). Some inscriptions in churches in townships and hamlets of Belmesthorpe, Casterton Magna, Casterton Parva, Empingham, Essendine, Hardwick, Horn, Inthorpe, Kelthorpe, Ketton, Pickworth, Ryhall, Tickencote, Tinwell, Tolethorpe, Woodhead

The Incised Slabs of Leicestershire & Rutland by F. A. Greenhill (1958) 191-206. Every church now or formerly containing incised slabs

BRAUNSTON Ch *Antiquarian Notes about Braunston & the Neighbourhood Thereof* by Rev. B. Barrett (1916) 84. Ch & extr Chyd *Rutland Magazine & County Historical Record* 5:39 (1910) 201
CALDECOT Ch & extr Chyd *Gent Mag* (1797) II, 817
CASTERTON, GREAT Chyd MS (1910)
CLIPSHAM Ch *Gent Mag* (1864) II, 762-763
COTTESMORE Ch & extr Chyd *Rutland Magazine & County Historical Record* 4:31 (1910) 200-201
DRY STOKE Ch *Gent Mag* (1864) II, 501
EXTON Ch *Rutland Magazine & County Historical Record* 3:23 (1908) 196-200; 3:24 (1908) 225-229
MARKET OVERTON Ch & extr Chyd *Rutland Magazine & County Historical Record* 4:28 (1909) 98-100
PRESTON Ch *Gent Mag* (1864) II, 500
RIDLINGTON Ch *Rutland Magazine &*

County Historical Record 2:13 (1906) 132-133
STRETTON Ch *Rutland Magazine & County Historical Record* 4:32 (1910) 232. Chyd MS (1910)
UPPINGHAM Ch *Gent Mag* (1864) II, 500-501; *Rutland Magazine & County Historical Record* 2:11 (1906) 69-71

SHROPSHIRE

The Deeds of Dudleston by Revd F. Brighton (1949) 173-185. Extracts, mainly only one per parish, from Astbury, Atcham, Burford, Cheswardine, Church Stretton, Cleobury, Clun, Colestay, Donnington, East Thorp, Edgmund, Ellesmere, High Ercall, Longmer, Ludlow, Madeley, Morville, Much Wenlock, Neen Solars, Onibury, Prees, Shifnal, Shrewsbury (St Giles, St Julian, St Mary), Westnor, Whiteladies, Whittington, Winnington.

ADDERLEY Chyd TS (1985)
ALBRIGHTON Ch *Gent Mag* (1794) II, 799-801; *SAS* 2 ser xi (1899) 144-147. Ch & Chyd TS (1981)
ASHFORD CARBONELL Ch TS (1985)
ASTLEY Ch & Chyd TS (1983)
ASTLEY ABBOTS Ch & Chyd TS (1984)
ATCHAM Ch *Gent Mag* (1806) II, 1001-1002, repr in *Salopian Shreds and Patches* 2 (1876) 53-54
BASCHURCH Ch & Chyd TS (1983)
BATTLEFIELD Ch & Chyd TS (1985)
BAYSTON HILL Chyd TS (1983)
BEDSTONE Ch & Chyd TS (1985)
BENTHALL Ch *Broseley and its Surroundings* by J. Rendall (1879) 313
BERRINGTON Ch *SAS* 1 ser iii (1880) 153-156
BERWICK Ch *SAS* 2 ser i (1889) 371-372
BETTON STRANGE Ch extr *SAS* 2 ser i (1889) 388-389
BICTON Ch & (extr) Chyd *SAS* 2 ser i (1889) 404-406
BILLINGSLEY Ch & Chyd TS (1981)
BITTERLEY Ch *Gent Mag* (1831) II, 297-298; (1863) I, 93-94. Chyd TS (1984)
BOMERE HEATH Methodist Chap & B.g. TS (1985). Presbyterian B.g. TS (1985)
BROSELEY Ch *Broseley and its Surroundings* by J. Rendall (1879) 190-197. Baptist B.g. TS (1975)
BROUGHTON Ch & Chyd TS (1980)
BURFORD Ch *Gent Mag* (1808) II, 984-985
CARDESTON Ch & Chyd TS (1981)
CEFN Y BLODWEL Chapel B.g. TS (1982)

CHELMARSH Ch & Chyd TS (1985)
CHORLEY Baptist Chapel Chap & B.g. TS (1981)
CLAVERLEY Ch extr *Gent Mag* (1822) II, 490-491
CLEE ST MARGARET Ch & Chyd TS (1985)
CLEOBURY MORTIMER Ch *SAS* 1 ser ii (1879) 64-70. Ch & Chyd TS (1945)
CLIVE Ch & Chyd TS (1982)
COALBROOKDALE Friends B.g. TS (1983)
COCKSHUTT Ch & Chyd TS (1983)
COLD WESTON Ch & Chyd TS (1985)
CONDOVER Chyd TS (1983)
COUND Ch extr *Gent Mag* (1820) II, 201-202, repr in *Salopian Shreds and Patches* 2 (1876) 37-38
COXALL Baptist Chap & B.g. TS (1985)
CRESSAGE Old & New Chyds TS (1985)
CRIFTINS Chyd TS (1982)
DIDDLEBURY Ch *SAS* 1 ser ix (1886) 291-295
DONINGTON Ch *SAS* 1 ser vi (1882) 3-13
DUDLESTON Chyd TS (1982); extr *The Deeds of Dudleston* by Revd F. Brighton (1949) 137-138
EATON UNDER HEYWOOD Ch & Chyd *SAS* 4 ser x (1925-6) xiv-xxii
EDSTASTON Ch & Chyd TS (1984)
ELLESMERE Ch *Coll Top et Gen* 3 (1836) 91-94
FAULS Chyd MS (1914)
FELTON, WEST Ch extr *SAS* 2 ser ix (1897) 347 376-379
FITZ Ch & Chyd TS (1982)
FRODESLEY Chyd TS (1984)
GLAZELEY Ch & Chyd TS (1981)
GRINSHILL Ch & Chyd TS (1981)
HALESOWEN Ch & Chyd extr *Gent Mag* (1803) II, 613-615 724
HANWOOD Ch & Chyd *SAS* 4 ser iii (1913) xv-xxxiv. Chyd *Shropshire Notes & Queries* 3 ser iii (1913) 48, 64 (repr from "The Shrewsbury Chronicle")
HARLEY Ch *SAS* 1 ser iv (1881) 331-336
HARMER HILL Chapel B.g. TS (1980)
HODNET Ch extr *Gent Mag* (1821) II, 394-395, repr in *Salopian Shreds and Patches* 2 (1876) 56. Hopton Methodist B.g. TS (1984)
HOPTON CASTLE Ch & Chyd TS (1985)
HOPTON WAFERS Ch *SAS* 3 ser ix (1909) 279-281
HORDLEY Ch & Chyd TS (1983)
JACKFIELD Chyd TS (1983)
KEMBERTON Ch & Chyd TS (1982)
KETLEY Chyd TS (1981)
KINNERSLEY Chyd TS (1985)
KNOCKIN HEATH Methodist B.g. TS (1985)
LEATON Ch *SAS* 2 ser vi (1894) 379-380. Ch &

Chyd TS (1981)

LEEBOTWOOD Ch extr *Gent Mag* (1831) I, 393-394

LEIGHTON Ch & Chyd *SAS* 1 ser vi (1883) 373-379

LILLESHALL Chyd TS (1985)

LLANYBLODWEL Chyd TS (1981)

LLANYMYNECH Chyd TS (1985)

LOPPINGTON Ch & Chyd TS (1980)

LUDLOW Ch *Gent Mag* (1808) II, 1142-1144; *The History and Antiquities of Ludlow* by T. Wright, 2nd edn. (1826) 153-155; *The History of Ludlow and its Neighbourhood* by T. Wright (1852) 464-469

MADELEY Chyd TS (1984)

MAESBROOK Chyd TS (1985)

MARKET DRAYTON Chyd TS (1985). Baptist Chapel B.g. TS (1981). Congregational Chapel B.g. TS (1982)

MARTON Ch & Chyd TS (1985)

MELVERLEY Chyd TS (1984)

MEOLE BRACE Ch & Chyd *SAS* 2 ser viii (1896) 127-130; TS (1984)

MIDDLETON SCRIVEN Ch & Chyd TS (1981)

MONTFORD Ch & Chyd TS (1982)

MORE Ch, Chyd & Cmy TS (1984)

MORETON CORBET Ch *SAS* 1 ser vii (1884) 315-320. Ch & Chyd TS (1985)

MORTON Chyd TS (1983)

MUNSLOW Ch *Gent Mag* (1833) I, 9-10

MYDDLE Ch & Chyd TS (1981)

NASH Ch MS (1914)

NEEN SOLLARS Ch MS (1914). Ch & Chyd *Gen* 3 (1879) 36-37

NESS, GREAT Ch *The Story of Great Ness* by Revd F. Brighton (1933) 47-49

NORBURY Ch & Chyd TS (1981)

OAKENGATES Chyd TS (1981)

OSWESTRY Ch *Gent Mag* (1810) I, 409-411. Ch & Chyd *The History of Oswestry* by W. Cathrall (1855) 138-148; *SAS* 1 ser vi (1883) 133-182

PETTON Ch TS (1982)

PITCHFORD Ch *SAS* 2 ser vii (1895) 375-380

PLOWDEN Private R.C. Cmy TS (1982)

PONTESBURY Ch extr *Gent Mag* (1827) I, 297-299; extr *SAS* 2 ser v (1893) 250-251

PRESTON GUBBALS Ch & Chyd TS (1980)

PRESTON ON THE WEALD MOORS Ch & Chyd TS (1985)

QUATFORD Ch extr *Gent Mag* (1818) I, 17

RATLINGHOPE Ch & Chyd TS (1982)

RICHARDS CASTLE St Bartholomew Ch & Chyd TS (1985). All Saints Ch TS (1985)

ROWTON Chyd TS (1985)

RUSHBURY Ch & Chyd TS (1985)

RUYTON IN THE ELEVEN TOWNS Ch *SAS* 2 ser viii (1896) 367-372. Ch & Chyd TS (1985)

ST MARTIN Ch & Chyd TS (1985)

SELATTYN Ch & Chyd extr *SAS* 2 ser vi (1894) 92-98

SHAWBURY Ch *SAS* 1 ser vii (1884) 303-304. Ch & Chyd TS (1985)

SHEINTON Old Chyd TS (1985)

SHERIFFHALES Ch *The Monumental Inscriptions in the Parish of Sheriffhales, including the Chapelry of Woodcote, co. Salop* by A. T. Tompson (1899)

SHIPTON Ch *SAS* 1 ser viii (1885) 461-466

SHREWSBURY Abbey Ch *Gent Mag* (1813) I, 306-308; TS (1982) from *A History of Shrewsbury* by H. Owen and J. B. Blakeway (1825). St Alkmund Ch extr *Gent Mag* (1794) II, 1086, (1796) I, 369-370; Ch & Chyd TS (1981 & 1982) from Owen & Blakeway; MS (1918) copied 1881. St Chad Ch & Chyd TS (1982) from Owen & Blakeway. St Giles Ch extr *Gent Mag* (1794) II, 694 909; Ch & Chyd TS (1982) from Owen & Blakeway. St Julian Ch & Chyd TS (1981 & 1983) from Owen & Blakeway; detached Chyd TS (1982). St Mary Ch & Chyd TS (1981 & 1982) from Owen & Blakeway

SIDBURY Ch & Chyd TS (1981)

SNEAD Ch & Chyd TS (1985)

STANTON ON HINE HEATH Ch & Chyd extr *SAS* 1 ser vii (1884) 332. Chyd TS (1985)

STIRCHLEY Chyd TS (1981)

STOCKTON Ch & Chyd TS (1981)

STOTTESDON Chyd TS (1981). Methodist Chapel B.g. TS (1981)

SUTTON BY SHREWSBURY Ch extr *SAS* 4 ser v (1915) 146-147

SUTTON MADDOCK Ch & Chyd TS (1981)

TASLEY Ch & Chyd TS (1983)

TELFORD Chyd TS (1977)

TIBBERTON Chyd TS (1985)

TONG Ch *SAS* 1 ser v (1882) 315-333; *A Guide to Tong Church, Shropshire* by G. Griffiths (1885); *A History of Tong, Shropshire* by G. Griffiths (1894) 30-94

TREFONEN Old & New Chyd & Chapel B.g. TS (1984)

UPPINGTON Ch & Chyd extr *SAS* 1 ser v (1882) 92-96

UPTON MAGNA Ch extr *SAS* 1 ser vi (1883) 362-364

WEM Aston Street Cmy TS (1982)

WESTON UNDER REDCASTLE Chyd & Cmy TS (1984)

WOMBRIDGE Chyd TS (1982)

WOODCOTE Ch *The Monumental Inscriptions in the Parish of Sheriffhales, including the*

Chapelry of Woodcote, co. Salop by A. T.
Tompson (1899)
WORFIELD Ch & Chyd TS (1985)
WROCKWARDINE Ch extr *SAS* 4 ser viii
(1920-21) 188 194 196 207-208
WROCKWARDINE WOOD Chyd TS (1981)
WROXETER Ch & Chyd TS (1985)

STAFFORDSHIRE

ADBASTON Ch & Chyd TS (1984)
ALDRIDGE Ch & (extr) Chyd *Notes and
Collections Relating to the Parish of Aldridge*
by J. Finch (1889) 41-45 105-112
ALREWAS Ch & Chyd TS (1984)
ALSTONFIELD Ch & Chyd TS (1982)
ANSLOW Chyd & New Cmy TS (1984)
ARMITAGE Independent B.g. (1906) *YOM* 4
ASTON, LITTLE Ch & Chyd TS (1984)
AUDLEY Ch *Gent Mag* (1813) II, 113-115
BARLASTON Old & New Chyds TS (1982)
BARTON UNDER NEEDWOOD see
TATENHILL
BETLEY Ch *Gent Mag* (1809) I, 521-522
BILSTON Swan Bank Wesleyan B.g. TS (1981)
copied 1964
BRAMSHALL Ch & Chyd TS (1983)
BREWOOD Ch & (extr) Chyd *Notes and
Collections Relating to Brewood* by W. Parke
(1860) 15-30
BROMWICH, WEST All Saints Ch & Chyd TS
(1982 & 1985). Christ Church Chyd TS (1984)
BROUGHTON see ECCLESHALL
BURSLEM St Paul Chyd TS (1980)
BURTON ON TRENT Baptist B.g. TS (1984)
CANNOCK Ch *Top* 2 (1790) 41-42. See also
HEATH HAYES
CANWELL Chyd TS (1984)
CHEADLE Ch & Chyd extr *History of Cheadle*
by R. Plant (1881) 79-90
CHRISTCHURCH ON NEEDWOOD Ch TS
(1985)
CODSALL Ch & Chyd TS (1984)
COLTON Ch & Chyd TS (1983)
COSELEY Ch *Annals of the Parish Church,
Coseley* by J. Mills (1912) 80-85
CROXTON Ch & Chyd TS (1985)
DARLASTON Ch *History of Darlaston* by F.
W. Hackwood (1887) 66-72; Ch & Chyd TS
(1981). St George Chyd TS (1981). Pinfold
Street Wesleyan B.g. TS (1981)
DENSTONE Ch & Chyd TS (1984)
DRAYTON BASSETT Chyd (1902) *YOM* 4
ECCLESHALL Ch Hearne IV, 5-7. Broughton
Chapel *ibid* 7-9

EDINGALE Chyd (1906) *YOM* 4
ELKSTONE Ch & Chyd TS (1980)
ETRURIA Chyd MS (1980)
FAREWELL Ch & Chyd TS (1983). Chyd
(1906) *YOM* 4
FAZELEY Ch & Chyd TS (1985)
FORTON Ch *Gent Mag* (1801) I, 17
GNOSALL Ch & Chyd TS (1985)
HANDSWORTH St Mary Ch *Top* 4 (1791)
254-255; *Gent Mag* (1794) II, 712-714; Ch &
Chyd TS (c. 1985). St Andrew Ch TS (1981).
St James Ch & Chyd TS (c. 1981). Union Row
Congregational B.g. TS (1981)
HANLEY Chyd TS (1980). St Jude Ch TS
(1982). Bethesda Methodist B.g. TS (1980)
HARLASTON Chyd (1906) *YOM* 4
HEATH HAYES Ch & Chyd TS (1982)
HOPWAS St Chad Ch & Chyd TS (1984). St
John Chyd TS (1984)
IPSTONES Ch *The Tale of Ipstones* by F.
Brighton (1937) 54-55 58-60
KEELE Ch *Gent Mag* (1811) II, 306-309. Ch &
Chyd TS (1982)
LICHFIELD Cathedral *Lichfield Cathedral – A
History of the Naval and Military Monuments,
Memorials and Colours* by M. B. Savage
(1945). St Chad Chyd (1906) *YOM* 4. St
Michael Chyd (1906) *YOM* 4
LONGTON Chyd TS (1980). St James Chyd TS
(1980) copied 1956
MADELEY Ch *Gent Mag* (1809) I, 409-411;
Madeley, Staffordshire by R. Nicholls (1935)
34-36
MAER Ch *Gent Mag* (1812) II, 505-506
NEWCASTLE UNDER LYME Ch & Chyd TS
(1983)
NEWTON SOLNAY Chyd TS (c. 1971)
NORTON UNDER CANNOCK Ch *Top* 2
(1790) 42-43
ONECOTE Ch & Chyd TS (1984)
OULTON Ch & Chyd TS (1984)
PENKHULL Ch & Chyd TS (1982)
PENKRIDGE Ch *Gent Mag* (1822) I, 592-594.
Ch & Chyd TS (1984)
PERRY BAR Chyd TS (c. 1950)
RUGELEY Old Ch & Chyd Hearne IV, 2-4;
Old Chyd (1906) *YOM* 4
SEDGLEY Ch & Chyd TS (1981). Vicarage
Street Chyd TS (n.d.)
SHARESHILL Chyd TS (1982)
SHEEN Ch & Chyd TS (1985)
SHENSTONE Chyd (1906) *YOM* 4
SMETHWICK Old Church Ch & Chyd TS
(1981)
STAFFORD Christ Church Ch & Chyd TS
(1984). [?parish] Ch Hearne IV, 4-5
STANDON Ch *History of Standon* by E. Salt

(1888) 158-164

STOKE ON TRENT Epworth Street Wesleyan Chapel TS (1984)

STONNALL Chyd TS (1984)

TAMWORTH Ch extr *Tamworth Parish Church* By H. C. Mitchell (1935) 175-186 214-217. Old Chyd (1906) *YOM* 4. Chyd TS (1957). Garden of Rest MS (n.d.)

TATENHILL Ch *A History of the Parish of Tatenhill* by Sir R. Hardy, vol 1 (1907) 16-17. Ch & Chyd TS (1985). St James, Barton Ch Hardy *ibid* 29

TETTENHALL Ch *A History of the Parish of Tettenhall* by J. P. Jones (1894) 252-260

UTTOXETER Ch *History of the Town of Uttoxeter* by F. Redfern (1865) 169-183

WALL Ch & Chyd TS (1982)

WALSALL Ch & Chyd TS (1982). Bath Street B.g. *Register of Inscriptions, Bath Street Burial Ground, Walsall* (Borough of Walsall, n.d.). St Mary's, The Mount R.C. Chyd TS (1981)

WATERFALL Ch & Chyd TS (1984)

WEDNESBURY Ch *History of Wednesbury* by J. Nock Bagnall (1854) 31-40

WEEFORD Ch & Chyd TS (1985)

WEST BROMWICH see BROMWICH, WEST

WHISTON Ch & Chyd TS (1985)

WHITTINGTON Chyd (1906) *YOM* 4

WILLENHALL Ch & Chyd MS (1980)

WOLSTANTON Ch *Gent Mag* (1811) II, 323-325

WOLVERHAMPTON St George Chyd TS (1981)

WOMBOURNE Ch & Chyd TS (1984)

WARWICKSHIRE

The Antiquities of Warwickshire by Sir William Dugdale (1730). A few MIs for each parish

The Mill Stephenson List of Monumental Brasses in the British Isles revised by the Monumental Brass Society (1977). About 130 parishes mentioned

ALDERMINSTER Ch & Chyd *Walks around Stratford* by Rev. H. Bloom (n.d.) 47-52

ALLESLEY Ch & Chyd TS of parish register (1972) i 155, ii 138-139

ALNE, GREAT Chyd MS (n.d.)

ALVERSTON Ch *Misc Gen et Her* 4 ser ii (1908) 106-109

ASHOW Ch & Chyd TS (1984)

ASTLEY Ch & Chyd TS (1982)

ASTON Chyd *YOM* 29; TS (1947); TS (1973); TS (1982)

ATHERSTONE Methodist Chap & B.g. TS (1985). United Reformed Chap & B.g. TS (1985)

ATHERSTONE-ON-STOUR Ch & Chyd *The Sepulchral Inscriptions of Warwickshire* 1 by Rev J. H. & Mary Bloom (1897)

ATTLEBOROUGH Chyd TS (1946)

AUSTREY Ch & Chyd TS (1981)

AVON DASSETT Chyd extr MS (n.d.)

BADDESLEY CLINTON Ch & Chyd TS (1984); Chyd MS (n.d.)

BAGINTON Ch & extr Chyd *Gent Mag* (1849) I, 28-29. Ch & Chyd TS (1984)

BARCHESTON Chyd MS (n.d.); MS (n.d.)

BARFORD Ch & extr Chyd MS (n.d.)

BARSTON Ch & Chyd TS (1981)

BARTLEY GREEN Chyd TS (1984)

BASCOTE HEATH Chyd TS (1984)

BAXTERLEY Ch & Chyd TS (1984). Chyd extr TS (1980)

BEARLEY Chyd TS (1985); MS (n.d.)

BEAUDESERT Ch & Chyd *The Records of Beaudesert, Henley-in Arden* by W. Cooper (1931) 47-57; TS (1982). Chyd MS (n.d.)

BENTLEY Chyd TS (1981)

BERKSWELL Ch *Gent Mag* (1827) I, 577-578. Ch & Chyd TS (1982). Chyd *YOM* 4

BERROW, OLD Ch & Chyd TS (1981)

BICKENHILL Ch & Chyd TS (1982). Chyd *YOM* 4

BILLESLEY Ch & Chyd TS (1978)

BINTON Chyd MS (1910)

BIRMINGHAM St Martin Chyd TS (1981). Christ Church *A History of the C. of E. Cemetery* by W. Wilson (1900) 34-62. St Bartholomew Chyd MS (n.d.). St Paul in the Field Chyd TS (1985). St Philip Chyd *Midland Antiquary* 3 (1884-5) 37-38 45-49 75 136-138. St Chad R.C. Cathedral Ch TS (1984). Old Meeting Chap & B.g. *Memorials of the Old Meeting House and Burial Ground* by C. H. Beale (1882). New Meeting Chap MS appendix (1913) to *Birmingham Free Christian Society* by A. B. Matthews (1900) 77-87. Kaye Hill Cemetery *YOM* 4. General Hospital TS (1986)

BISHOPS ITCHINGTON Ch & Chyd TS (1984)

BISHOPS TACHBROOK Ch & Chyd TS (1984)

BORDESLEY Ch & Chyd TS (1975). Chyd TS (1980)

BOURTON-ON-DUNSMORE Chyd TS (1983)

BRAILES Ch & Chyd MS (1914). Chyd MS (n.d.)

BRINKLOW Ch & Chyd TS (1984). Chyd *YOM* 4

BUBBENHALL Ch & Chyd TS (1985)
BULKINGTON Ch & Chyd TS (1981). Chyd
TS (n.d.)
BURMINGTON Ch & Chyd MS (1914). Chyd
TS (1985)
BURTON DASSET Chyd MS (n.d.)
BUTLERS MARSTON Chyd MS (n.d.)
CASTLE BROMWICH Ch & Chyd TS (1986)
CHADSHUNT Chyd MS (1911)
CHARLECOTE Ch & Chyd TS (1982). Chyd
MS (n.d.)
CHERINGTON Ch & Chyd TS (1985). Chyd
MS (n.d.)
CHESTERTON Chyd MS (1911)
CLIFFORD CHAMBERS Ch & Chyd TS
(1981). See also GLOUCESTERSHIRE
CLIFTON-UPON-DUNSMORE Ch & Chyd
TS (1977)
COLESHILL Chyd extr MS (n.d.); *YOM* 29.
Chyd & Old Cmy TS (1983)
COMPTON, LONG Chyd MS (1910)
COMPTON VERNEY Ch & Chyd *Frag Gen* 5
(1900) 14-25; *Historical Notes on Compton
Verney Church* by E. M. Mills (1932)
COMPTON WYNIATES Ch & Chyd TS
(1984). Chyd MS (1918)
CORLEY Ch & Chyd TS (1984)
COUGHTON Chyd MS (n.d.)
COVENTRY Cathedral Ch *The Monumental
Inscriptions in the Parish Church of St
Michael, Coventry* by J. Astley (1884); Chyd
TS (n.d.) St John the Baptist Ch & Chyd TS
(1981). West Orchard Congregational B.g. MS
(n.d.); TS (1984)
DUNCHURCH Ch & Chyd *Gent Mag* (1795)
II, 988-989. Baptist B.g. TS (1984)
EASTERN GREEN Chyd TS (1984)
EDGBASTON St Augustine Ch TS (1982). St
Bartholomew Ch & Chyd TS (1985). St
George Ch TS (1984); Ch & extr Chyd *Gent
Mag* (1825) I, 393-394
ELMDON Ch (Spooner family) *Frag Gen* 7
(1902) 57-62. Ch & Chyd TS (1980)
ERDINGTON Congregational B.g. TS (c. 1985)
ETTINGTON Holy Trinity Ch *Lower
Eatington, its Manor House & Church* by E.
P. Shirley (1869) 60-73; *Walks around
Stratford* by Rev H. Bloom (n.d.) 41-43 63; TS
(1981); Chyd (1985). St Thomas a Beckett
Chyd TS (1981)
EXHALL Chyd TS (1967)
FARNBOROUGH Chyd MS (1913)
FENNY COMPTON Ch & Chyd TS (1981)
FOLESHILL Ch & Chyd TS (1976)
FRANKTON Ch & Chyd TS (1983)
GAYDON Chyd TS (1981)
GRANDBOROUGH Ch & Chyd TS (1981)

GRENDON Chyd *YOM* 4
HAMPTON-IN-ARDEN Ch & Chyd TS
(1982). Ch & extr Chyd *Hampton-in-Arden, a
Warwickshire Village* by J. C. Adams (1951)
33-38 90-91. Chyd MS (1913)
HAMPTON LUCY Chyd (n.d.)
HAMPTON ON THE HILL R.C. Chyd TS
(1982)
HANDSWORTH see STAFFORDSHIRE
HATTON Ch *Gent Mag* (1805) II, 995-996;
Misc Gen et Her 5 ser i (1916) 318-319
HENLEY-IN-ARDEN Ch *Henley-in-Arden* by
W. Cooper (1946) 60-62; TS (1982)
HOCKLEY All Saints Chyd TS (1984). St
George in the Fields Chyd TS (1975)
HONILEY Ch & Chyd TS (n.d.). Chyd MS
(1981)
HUNNINGHAM Ch & Chyd TS (1984)
HURLEY Ch TS (1985)
IDLICOTE Chyd MS (n.d.)
KENILWORTH Ch TS (1982). Chyd TS
(1982); MS (n.d.). R.C. Chyd TS (1982)
KERESLEY Ch & Chyd TS (1982)
KINGSBURY Ch & Chyd TS (1984). Chyd
YOM 4
KINGS HEATH Ch & Chyd TS (1984)
KINGS NORTON Ch *The History of Kings
Norton & Northfield Wards* by A. B. Lock
(1938) 119-121
KNOWLE Ch *Gent Mag* (1793) I, 420-422; Ch
& extr Chyd *The Collegiate Church of Ss
John the Baptist, Laurence & Anne of Knowle*
by A. A. Upton (1966) 31-38 116-118.
Chadwick End R.C. Chyd TS (1981); TS (n.d.)
LAPWORTH Ch & Chyd TS (1981-85)
LEA MARSTON Chyd MS (1984)
LEAMINGTON All Saints Ch & extr Chyd TS
(1983); Ch & Chyd MS (n.d.); Chyd MS
(n.d.). New Street Cmy TS (1983). Leam
Terrace Cmy TS (1983)
LEEK WOOTTON Ch & Chyd TS (1984)
LIGHTHORNE Chyd MS (1911)
LOXLEY Ch & Chyd *Walks Around Stratford*
by Rev J. H. Bloom (n.d.) 70-72
LOZELLS Ch TS (1983)
MANCETTER Chyd *YOM* 4; TS (n.d.)
MARTON Chyd TS (1985)
MAXSTOKE Chyd TS (1982); TS (1985); *YOM*
29
MEREVALE Ch & Chyd TS (1985)
MERIDEN Ch & Chyd & New B.g. TS (1983)
MILVERTON, OLD Ch & Chyd TS (1986)
MORETON MORELL Chyd MS (n.d.)
MORTON BAGOT Ch *Warwickshire People &
Places* by J. Burman (1936) 31-32. Ch & Chyd
MS (n.d.)
MOSELEY Chyd TS (1976)

NEWBOLD PACY Chyd MS (1910)
NUNEATON Chyd *YOM* 4
NUTHURST CUM HOCKLEY HEATH Ch
The Story of Nuthurst cum Hockley Heath by
J. J. Belton (1948) 21-22. Chyd TS (1982)
OLTON Chyd TS (1982)
OXHILL Chyd MS (n.d.)
PACKINGTON, GREAT Chyd *YOM* 29
PACKINGTON, LITTLE Chyd *YOM* 29
PACKWOOD Ch *The Story of Packwood* by J.
J. Belton (1951) 17-19 68-71 74-77
PILLERTON HERSEY Ch & Chyd TS (1984).
Chyd MS (n.d.)
PILLERTON PRIORS Chyd TS (1983)
POLESWORTH Chyd *YOM* 4. Baptist Chap &
B.g. TS (1985)
PRESTON BAGOT Ch & Chyd TS (1982)
PRIORS SALFORD Ch TS (1978)
ROWINGTON Ch & Chyd TS (1985)
RUGBY Chyd TS (1976); TS (1977)
SALTLEY Chyd xerox of MS index (1977)
SHERBORNE Chyd TS (1981)
SHIPSTON-UPON-STOUR Ch & Chyd *Local
Notes reprinted from Stratford-on-Avon
Herald* (n.d.) 23-28
SHIRLEY Chyd TS (1985)
SHOTTESWELL Chyd MS (1911)
SHUSTOKE Chyd extr TS (n.d.)
SOLIHULL Ch Hearne IV, 1-2. Chyd TS
(1985)
SOUTHAM Chyd MS (n.d.)
SPERNALL Ch *Warwickshire People & Places*
by J. Burman (1936) 4-6. Chyd MS (n.d.)
STIVICHALL Ch & Chyd TS (1981)
STOCKINGFORD Ch & Chyd TS (1981-85)
STONELEIGH Ch & Chyd TS (1981)
STRATFORD-UPON-AVON Ch & extr Chyd
*Shakespeare's Church; otherwise the
Collegiate Church of The Holy Trinity,
Stratford-upon-Avon* by J. Harvey Bloom
(1902) 147-254 276-277
STRETTON-UNDER-FOSSE B.g. xerox of
MS (1983)
SUTTON COLDFIELD Holy Trinity Ch
History of Sutton Coldfield by Rev. W. K. R.
Bedford (1981) 70-73; Ch & Chyd TS (1985).
St James, Four Oaks Chyd extr *Midland
Ancestor* 6:7 (1982) 229
SUTTON-UNDER-BRAILES Chyd MS
(n.d.)
TANWORTH Ch *Warwickshire People &
Places* by J. Burman (1936) 71-72. Chyd TS
(1984)
TEMPLE BALSALL Ch & Chyd TS (1981).
Rabbit Lane Cmy TS (1981)
TEMPLE GRAFTON Chyd MS (n.d.)
TREDINGTON Ch & Chyd TS (1983)

TYSOE Chyd *The Parish Registers of Tysoe,
Warks* ed. by D. B. Woodfield (1976) xxxiii-
xliii 259-262; MS (n.d.)
UFTON Chyd MS (n.d.)
ULLENHALL Ch & Chyd TS (1982)
UMBERSLADE Baptist Chap & B.g. TS (1981)
WALMLEY Ch & Chyd TS (1984)
WALSGRAVE Cmy MS/TS (1957)
WAPPENBURY Ch & Chyd TS (1984). R.C.
Ch & Chyd TS (1986)
WARD END Ch & Chyd TS (1981)
WARMINGTON Ch & Chyd TS (1981). Chyd
extr MS (n.d.)
WARWICK Ch *Notices of the Church of St.
Mary & the Beauchamp Chapel* by H. T.
Cooke (1845) 45-53; Ch & Chyd TS (1982). St
Paul Ch & Chyd TS (1982)
WATER ORTON Ch, Chyd & Old Chyd TS
(1982)
WEDDINGTON Ch & Chyd MS (1917). Chyd
TS (1946)
WELLESBOURNE Ch & Chyd xerox of TS
(1977). Chyd MS (n.d.)
WESTON UNDER WETHERLEY Ch & Chyd
TS (1984)
WESTON UPON AVON Ch & Chyd TS (1985)
WESTWOOD HEATH Ch & Chyd TS (1984)
WHICHFORD Chyd MS (n.d.)
WHITACRE, OVER Chyd TS (1982)
WHITCHURCH Ch & Chyd *Walks around
Stratford* by Rev J. H. Bloom (n.d.) 7-11
WHITNASH Ch & Chyd TS (1981)
WILMCOTE Congregational B.g. TS (1978)
WIXFORD Ch & extr Chyd *Gen* 1 (1877) 15-19
WOLFHAMPCOTE Ch *Wolfhampcote
Registers* by E. R. Reid-Smith (1954) 123-131
WOLSTON Ch & Chyd & Baptist B.g. TS
(1984)
WOLVEY Ch & Chyd TS (1981)
WOOD END Ch TS (1985)
WOOTTON WAWEN Ch *Wootton Wawen, its
History & Records* by W. Cooper (1936) 108-
118. R.C. Chyd TS (1981)
WROXALL Ch, Chyd & Cmy TS (1981)
YARDLEY WOOD Chyd TS (1985)

WESTMORLAND

*Westmorland Church Notes: being the
Heraldry, Epitaphs & other Inscriptions in the
Thirty-two Ancient Parish Churches &
Churchyards of that County* by Edward
Bellasis (1888-9). Appleby St Lawrence,
Appleby St Michael, Asby, Askham,
Bampton, Barton, Beetham, Brough,

Brougham, Burton in Kendal, Cliburn, Clifton, Crosby Garret, Crosby Ravensworth, Dufton, Grasmere, Heversham, Kendal, Kirkby Lonsdale, Kirkby Stephen, Kirkby Thore, Long Marton, Lowther, Morland, Musgrave, Newbiggin, Ormside, Orton, Ravenstonedale, Shap, Warcop, Windermere

GRASMERE Ch & Chyd *Misc Gen et Her* NS iii (1880) 145-146 153-156 188

KENDAL Market Place B.g. *The Older Nonconformity in Kendal* by F. Nicholson & E. Axon (1915) 495-498

KIRKBY LONSDALE Ch & extr Chyd *The Story of the Church of St Mary the Virgin* by A. Pearson (1940) 30-32

MARDALE Ch & Chyd extr *Gen* NS 32 (1916) 222-227

MARTINDALE Ch & Chyd extr *Martindale Registers & Notes* by H. Brierley (1907) 100-102

ORTON Ch & Chyd TS (1977)

RAVENSTONEDALE Chap & B.g. *The High Chapel, Ravenstonedale* by C. C..E. Woodger (1955) 154 ff.

SHAP Chyd TS (1980)

TROUTBECK Chyd TS (n.d.)

WORCESTERSHIRE

ABBERLEY Ch & Chyd Bloom's Worcs MIs (n.d.)

ABBERTON Ch & Chyd TS (1986)

ABBOTS MORTON Chyd Bloom's Worcs MIs (n.d.)

ALDERMINSTER Ch & Chyd *Walks Round Stratford* by J. H. Bloom (n.d.) 46-52

ALVECHURCH Ch & Chyd TS (1986)

AMBLECOAT Ch & Chyd TS (1985)

ARELEY KINGS Ch & Chyd Bloom's Worcs MIs (n.d.)

BAYTON Ch & Chyd Bloom's Worcs MIs (1914)

BEDWARDINE see WORCESTER

BELBROUGHTON Ch & Chyd *Gent Mag* (1805) I, 505-506

BENGEWORTH Ch & Chyd Bloom's Worcs MIs (1917)

BEOLEY Ch & Chyd TS (1981)

BEWDLEY Ch Bloom's Worcs MIs (1914). Baptist B.g. Bloom's Worcs MIs (1915). Unitarian B.g. Bloom's Worcs MIs (1915)

BLOCKLEY Ch & Chyd *History of Blockley* by A. J. Soden (1875) 38-67. Chyd Bloom's Worcs MIs (1917)

BRADLEY WITH STOCK GREEN Ch & Chyd TS (1986). Stock Green Baptist B.g. TS (1986)

BREDICOT Ch & Chyd TS (1986)

BROMSGROVE Ch & Chyd TS (1983). Finstall B.g. TS (1983). Chapel Lane B.g. TS (1984)

BROOME Ch & Chyd TS (1981)

BROUGHTON HACKETT Ch & Chyd TS (1986)

BUSHLEY Ch & Chyd TS (1983)

CHURCHILL, near WORCESTER Ch Bloom's Worcs MIs (1917). Ch & Chyd TS (1986)

CHURCH HONEYBOURNE Ch Bloom's Worcs MIs (1917)

CHURCH LENCH Chyd Bloom's Worcs MIs (1917)

CLAINES St John the Baptist Ch, Chyd & Cmy TS (1982). Barbourne St George Ch & Chyd Bloom's Worcs MIs (1915); TS (1980). Barbourne St Mary Magdalene Ch Bloom's Worcs MIs (1915)

CLEEVE PRIOR Ch & Chyd TS (1984)

COOKHILL MANOR *Frag Gen* 7 (1902) 141-143

COFTON HACKETT Ch Hearne III, 152-153

DROITWICH St Andrew Ch & Chyd TS (1986). St Mary Chyd TS (1984). St Nicholas Ch & Chyd TS (1984)

DUDLEY St Thomas Ch & Chyd TS (1983). St James the Great Ch & Chyd TS (1976). R.C. Chyd TS (1975). Central Methodist B.g. (1979). Independent B.g. TS (1985)

EVESHAM All Saints Chyd *Evesham Churchyard Inscriptions* by E. A. R. Barnard (1899); Bloom's Worcs MIs (1914); TS (1970). St Lawrence Chyd Bloom's Worcs MIs (1915); TS (1970). Baptist Chap & B.g. TS (1985). Unitarian Chap & B.g. (1985). Friends B.g. TS (1985)

FLYFORD FLAVELL Ch & Chyd TS (1986)

FRANKLEY Chyd TS (1982)

GRAFTON FLYFORD Ch & Chyd TS (1986)

HAGLEY Ch & Chyd Bloom's Worcs MIs (1917). Chyd MS (1922)

HAMPTON Chyd TS (1986)

HANLEY WILLIAM Ch *Gen* I (1877) 215-217. Chyd *Gen* NS 6 (1877) 240-241

HUDDINGTON Ch & Chyd TS (1985)

KIDDERMINSTER St Mary Chyd Bloom's Worcs MIs (n.d.). St George Ch Bloom's Worcs MIs (n.d.)

KINGS NORTON Chyd TS (1946)

KYREWYARD Ch *Gen* I (1877) 181-183

LEIGH Chyd Bloom's Worcs MIs (1917)

LINDRIDGE Ch & Chyd MS (1964)

LITTLETON, NORTH & MIDDLE Ch &
Chyd TS (1981)
LITTLETON, SOUTH Ch & Chyd TS (1982)
LONGDON Ch & Chyd TS (1982)
MALVERN, GREAT Ch & Chyd Bloom's
Worcs MIs (1917)
MAMBLE Ch & Chyd *Gen* NS 7 (1891) 113-
115. Chyd Bloom's Worcs MIs (1914)
MITTON, LOWER Ch & Chyd Bloom's Worcs
MIs (1917)
OMBERSLEY Ch Bloom's Worcs MIs (1917)
PEDMORE Chyd TS (1982)
PENSAX Ch & Chyd TS (1965)
PENSETT Ch extr & Chyd TS (1983)
PEOPLETON Chyd TS (1982)
PERSHORE Holy Cross (Abbey) Ch & Chyd
Bloom's Worcs MIs (1917). St Andrew Chyd
Bloom's Worcs MIs (n.d.)
QUEENHILL Ch & Chyd TS (1980)
REDDITCH Evesham Street Congregational
B.g. *Midland Ancestor* 4 (1975-78) 84-85; TS
(1978)
SAPEY, UPPER Ch & Chyd TS (1983)
SHELSLEY BEAUCHAMP Ch & Chyd TS
(1967). Chyd *Gen* 3 (1879) 208-211
SHELSEY WALSH Ch *Gen* 2 (1878) 347-348
SHIPSTON-ON-STOUR Chyd Bloom's Worcs
MIs (1911)
SPETCHLEY Chyd Bloom's Worcs MIs (1917)
STANFORD ON TEME Ch & Chyd TS (1968)
STOCKTON ON TEME Ch & Chyd TS (1970)
STOKE PRIOR Ch & Chyd TS (1982)
STOURBRIDGE Ch & extr Chyd TS (1984).
Presbyterian Chap & B.g. TS (1985)
SWINFORD, OLD Ch Hearne III, 149 151-152
TENBURY Ch & Chyd Bloom's Worcs MIs
(1917)
THROCKMORTON Ch & Chyd TS (1986)
TIBBERTON Ch & Chyd TS (1986)
TIDMINGTON Ch & Chyd Bloom's Worcs
MIs (1917)
UPTON ON SEVERN Chyd TS (1985)
UPTON SNODSBURY Ch & Chyd TS (1986)
UPTON WARREN TS (1984)
WARNDON Ch & Chyd TS (1986)
WITLEY, GREAT Ch & Chyd TS (1968)
WOLLASTON Ch & Chyd TS (1983)
WORCESTER Cathedral *The Cathedral
Church of Worcester, Its Monuments & Their
Stories* by W. M. Ede (1925); *A Guide to
Monuments in Worcester Cathedral* by A.
Macdonald (1947); Old B.g. Bloom's Worcs
MIs (n.d.). St Andrew Ch Bloom *ibid.* St
Clement Chyd Bloom *ibid.* St Helen Ch & extr
Chyd Bloom *ibid.* St John Bedwardine Chyd
Bloom *ibid.* St Martin Ch & extr Chyd Bloom
ibid. St Michael Bedwardine Ch Bloom *ibid.*

St Nicholas Ch Bloom *ibid.* St Oswald's
Hospital Chyd Bloom *ibid.* St Peter the Great
Ch & Chyd Bloom *ibid.* St Swithin Ch Bloom
ibid. Tallow Hill B.g. Bloom *ibid.* St George,
Sansom Place R.C. Ch & Chyd Bloom *ibid.*
Angel Street Congregational Chap & B.g.
Bloom *ibid.* Friends B.g. Bloom *ibid.* Countess
of Huntingdons Chap Bloom *ibid; Misc Gen
et Her* 5 ser iv (1920-22) 190. For
BARBOURNE see CLAINES
WRIBBENHALL Chyd TS (1946)
WYCHBOLD Ch & Chyd TS (1986)
WYTHALL Ch & Chyd TS (1981). Kingswood
Meeting House Chap & B.g. TS (1981)

YORKSHIRE

Yorkshire Church Notes, 1619-1631 by Roger
Dodsworth. (Y.A.S. Record Series, vol 34,
1904)

ACASTER MALBIS Ch & Chyd TS (1976)
ACKLAM Chyd TS (1984)
ACOMB Ch & Chyd TS (1975)
ADEL Ch & Chyd *Registers of the Parish
Church of Adel, in the County of York, from
1606-1812 & Monumental Inscriptions* by G.
D. Lumb (Thoresby Soc. 5 (1895) 205-213)
ALDINGFLEET Ch Bloom's Yorks MSS vol 7,
28-29 (copied 1892). Ch & Chyd TS (1983)
ADWICK LE STREET Ch Bloom's Yorks
MSS vol 6, 89-91, vol 7, 167-168, (copied
1891-2). Ch & Chyd TS (1981)
AIRMYN Ch & Chyd TS (1985)
ALMONDBURY Ch & Chyd *Annals of the
Church of Almondbury* by C. A. Hulbert
(1882) 38-66 535-580. Cmy *Supplementary
Annals of the Church & Parish of
Almondbury* by C. A. Hulbert (1885) 138-162
ARDSLEY Ch Bloom's Yorks MSS vol 7, 15-
16 (copied 1892)
ARKSEY Ch Bloom's Yorks MSS vol 7, 220
(copied 1891). Ch & Chyd TS (1982)
ARMLEY Chyd TS (1978)
ASKERN Ch & Chyd TS (1981)
ASKRIGG Ch, Chyd & B.g. TS (1978)
AUSTERFIELD Chyd MS (1911)
BAINBRIDGE Quaker B.g. TS (1978)
BARNSLEY St Mary Churchfields Chyd TS
(n.d.)
BARTON Ch & Chyd TS (1980)
BARWICK-IN-ELMET Ch & Chyd *Wills,
Registers & Monumental Inscriptions in the
Parish of Barwick-in-Elmet* by G. D. Lumb
(1908) 418-425
BATLEY Ch Bloom's Yorks MSS vol 6, 105-

107 (copied 1891)
BAWTRY Ch & Chyd TS (1985)
BILBOROUGH Ch & Chyd TS (1974)
BIRSTALL Wesleyan B.g. TS (1975)
BISHOP BURTON Ch & Chyd TS (1985)
BISHOPTHORPE Old Ch & Chyd MS & TS (1977)
BOYNTON Ch Bloom's Yorks MSS vol 7, 222-223 (copied 1892)
BRADFORD Ch extr *The Bradford Antiquary* O.S. 1 (1888) 51-52 107-109 233-234; 2 (1895) 28-32. Ch & Chyd *The Churches of Yorkshire 1* by W. H. Hatton (1880) 95-96 105-108 129-132. Unitarian Chapel & B.g. TS (1938)
BRAMHAM Ch Bloom's Yorks MSS vol 7, 34 149-151
BRAMHOPE Puritan B.g. TS (1975)
BRAMLEY Methodist B.g. TS (1977)
BRANTINGHAM Ch & Chyd TS (1986). See also ELLERKER
BRANTON GREEN Private B.g. (Inchboard Family) TS (1975)
BRAYTON Ch Bloom's Yorks MSS vol 7, 130-133 (copied 1892)
BRIDLINGTON Ch Bloom's Yorks MSS vol 6, 129-132 (copied 1891)
BRIGHOUSE See RASTRICK
BROTHERTON Ch Bloom's Yorks MSS vol 7, 134-135 (copied 1892)
BURGHWALLIS Ch & Chyd TS (1983)
BURLEY IN WHARFEDALE Salem U.R.C. B.g. TS (1973)
BYLAND, OLD Ch & Chyd TS (1969)
CALVERLEY Ch *Registers of the Parish Church of Calverley* by Samuel Margerison 2 (1883) 40-48; *Memorials of Calverley Church* by H. Stapleton (n.d.) 283-287
CAMPSALL Chyd Bloom's Yorks MSS vol 7, 23-24 copied 1892)
CANTLEY Ch & Chyd Bloom's Yorks MSS vol. 7, 282-288 (copied 1892)
CAVE, NORTH Ch Bloom's Yorks MSS vol 6, 136-137 (copied 1891)
CAWTHORNE Chyd extr MS (1911)
CHAPEL ALLERTON Ch & Chyd *The Church in Chapel Allerton* by G. E. Kirk (1949) 44-45 54-55
CLECKHEATON Ch *The Churches of Yorkshire 1* by W. H. Hatton (1880) 5-6. Providence Place B.g. TS (1975)
COATHAM Ch & Chyd TS (1984). Chyd MS (1953)
COLD KIRBY Ch & Chyd TS (1969)
COVERHAM Chyd TS (1970)
COWTHORPE Ch & Chyd TS (1976)
CRAKEHALL Chyd MS (1971)
CRATHORNE Ch & Chyd TS (1985). Chyd TS (1984)

DALBY Ch & Chyd MS (1913)
DARFIELD Ch Bloom's Yorks MSS vol 7, 177-181 (copied 1890)
DENHOLME Wesleyan B.g. TS (n.d.)
DEWSBURY West Town Chyd TS (1975). Friends B.g. TS (1975). Longcauseway U.R.C. B.g. TS (1975)
DONCASTER *Ancient Memorial Brasses Remaining in the Deanery of Doncaster* by F. R. Fairbank (n.d.). Christ Church Ch Bloom's Yorks MSS vol 7, 210-211 (copied 1892). St George Ch Bloom's Yorks MSS vol 7, 119 212 (copied 1892). Cmy extr MS (1910)
DUNNINGTON Chyd TS (1970)
EASBY Ch & Chyd TS (1978)
EASINGTON Ch, Chyd & Cmy TS (1984)
ECCLESALL Ch Bloom's Yorks MSS vol 6, 26-27 (copied 1891)
ECCLESFIELD Ch Bloom's Yorks MSS vol 7, 182-190 (copied 1892)
ELLAND Chyd TS (1972). Huddersfield Road Chapel & B.g. TS (1969). Providence Chapel B.g. TS (1969)
ELLERKER Ch & Chyd TS (1986)
ELVINGTON Chyd TS (1970)
EMLEY Ch Bloom's Yorks MSS vol 6, 155-157 (copied 1891)
ESCRICK Chyd TS (1970)
ESTON Cmy TS (1975)
FANGFOSS Chyd TS (1970)
FARNHAM Ch & Chyd TS (1981)
FELKIRK Ch *The Churches of Yorkshire 1* by W. H. Hatton (1880) 109-110 124-126. Ch & Chyd Bloom's Yorks MSS vol 7, 116 272-280 (copied 1892)
FENWICK Chyd TS (1981)
FERRIBY, NORTH Chyd xerox of MS (1963)
FEWSTON Ch & Chyd TS (1978)
FINNINGLEY Ch & Chyd TS (1985). Chyd TS (1971)
FISHLAKE Ch & Chyd TS (1981)
FRICKLEY Ch & Chyd TS (1985)
FRODINGHAM, NORTH Ch & Chyd TS (1980)
FRYSTONE, MONK Ch Bloom's Yorks MSS vol 7, 138-140 (copied 1892)
FULFORD Chyd TS (1974)
GAYLE Sandemanian B.g. xerox of MS (1973); TS (1978)
GISBURN Chyd MS (1907)
GIVENDALE, GREAT Ch & Chyd TS (1979); TS (1982)
GOMERSAL Grove Independent B.g. TS (1976)
GOOLE Chyd TS (1964)
GREENHOW Ch & Chyd TS (1982)
GRINTON Ch extr *Gent Mag* (1813) II, 105-106

GUISBOROUGH Friends B.g. TS (1983)
GUISLEY Ch *The Churches of Yorkshire 1* by
W. H. Hatton (1880) 16. Methodist B.g. TS
(1978)
HACKNESS Ch Hearne IV, 241-243
HALBECK Balm Lane B.g. MS (1977)
HALIFAX *Little Known Graveyards* by
Halifax Antiquarian Soc. (1971). Ch *The
Monumental & Other Inscriptions in Halifax
Parish Church* by E. W. Crossley (1909). Ch &
Chyd extr *The Antiquities of the Town of
Halifax in Yorkshire* by Rev. T. Wright (1738)
79-88. Holy Trinity Ch & Chyd TS (1969). St
James Chyd TS (1974). Halifax Square
Congregational B.g. TS (1970). South Parade
Wesleyan B.g. TS (1970). Salem Chapel,
North Parade B.g. TS (1969). Pellon Lane B.g.
Pellon Lane Baptist Graveyard Inscriptions by
R. Bretton (1952)
HAREWOOD Ch *The History & Antiquities of
Harewood* by J. Jones (1859) 107-128
HARROGATE St. Luke Ch TS (1980)
HAWES Ch & Chyd TS (1978). Quaker B.g. TS
(1978)
HAWNBY Ch & Chyd TS (1969)
HAXBY Chyd MS (1910)
HAYWOOD Chyd TS (1980)
HAZLEWOOD Ch & Chyd TS (1974)
HEALAUGH Ch & Chyd TS (1975)
HEBDEN BRIDGE Burchcliffe Baptist B.g.
extr MS (1980)
HECKMONDWIKE Westgate Congregational
B.g. TS (1976). Upper Independent Chapel
B.g. TS (1980)
HEMINGBROUGH Ch & extr Chyd *The
History of Hemingbrough* by T. Burton (1888)
31-41
HEMSWORTH Chyd Bloom's Yorks MSS vol
7, 63-78 (copied 1914)
HILTON-IN-CLEVELAND Chyd TS (1976)
HINDERWELL Chyd TS (1984)
HIPPERHOLME Methodist B.g. *Little Known
Graveyards* by L. Morgan (1970). Independent
B.g. *ibid*
HOLMFIRTH Chyd *The History &
Topography of the Parish of Kirkburton* by H.
J. Morehouse (1861) 165-167. Chyd TS (1979).
Wesleyan Methodist Chapel & B.g.
Morehouse *op. cit.* 224-225
HONLEY Chyd TS (1975). Moorbottom B.g.
extr TS (1975)
HORBURY Chyd TS (1977)
HOTHAM Ch & Chyd TS (1986)
HULL Holy Trinity, Castle Street B.g. TS
(1985)
HUNSLET MOOR Ch TS (1974)
HUNTINGTON Chyd MS (1910)
ILKLEY Ch *The Churches of Yorkshire 1*

(1880) 12 21-22; extr *Misc Gen et Her* 2 (1876)
371-377. Ch & Chyd extr *Ilkley Ancient &
Modern* by R. Collyer & J. H. Turner (1885)
170-173. Middleton Hall Chapel *Cath Rec Soc*
4 (1907) 429-430
ILLINGWORTH Ch *The Story of St. Mary's,
Illingworth* by G. R. Oakley (1924) 134-135.
Chyd extr TS (1973)
JACKSON BRIDGE Wesleyan Methodist B.g.
*The History & Topography of the Parish of
Kirkburton* by H. J. Morehouse (1861)
201-201
KEIGHLEY Ch *The Churches of Yorkshire 1*
by W. H. Hatton (1880) 55-56; MS (1911)
KELLINGTON Ch extr *Gent Mag* (1831) II,
15-16
KETTLEWELL Methodist B.g. TS (1979)
KEXBY Chyd TS (1970)
KILNHURST Ch & Chyd TS (1981)
KILNSEA Ch & Chyd TS (1982)
KINGCROSS Chyd TS (1975)
KIPPAX Ch Bloom's Yorks MSS vol 6, 87-88
(copied 1891)
KIRK BRAMWITH Ch & Chyd TS (1983)
KIRKBURTON Ch & Chyd *The History &
Topography of the Parish of Kirkburton* by H.
J. Morehouse (1861) 70-74
KIRKLEATHAM Chyd MS (1976)
KIRKLEVINGTON Chyd TS (1976)
KIRK SMEATON Chyd Bloom's Yorks MSS
vol 7, 78-79 (copied 1892)
KIRKTHORPE Ch & Chyd Bloom's Yorks
MSS vol 6, 158-161 (copied 1891)
KNOTTINGLEY Ch Bloom's Yorks MSS vol
7, 12-14 (copied 1892)
LEDSHAM Ch Bloom's Yorks MSS vol 7, 155-
157 (copied 1892)
LEEDS St Peter Ch Bloom's Yorks MSS vol 6,
61-82 (copied 1891); MS (n.d.); Ch & Chyd
extr *Thoresby Soc.* 2 (1891) 26-32 41-42; Chyd
ibid 24 (1919) 256-276; 26 (1924) 41-60. St
John Ch & Chyd *ibid* 33 (1935) 306-426
(copied 1900); extr *ibid* 2 (1891) 33-35
LIGHTCLIFFE Ch *The Churches of Yorkshire
1* by W. H. Hatton (1880) 24
LIVERTON Chyd TS (1983)
LOCKINGTON Ch & Chyd TS (1983)
LOCKWOOD Rehoboth Baptist B.g. TS (1977)
LOWTHORPE Ch & Chyd TS (1979)
LUND Ch & Chyd TS (1983)
LYDGATE (HOLMFIRTH) Unitarian Chapel
& B.g. *The History & Topography of the
Parish of Kirkburton* by H. J. Morehouse
(1861) 191-192; B.g. TS (1979)
MARR Ch & Chyd TS (1983)
MARSKE Chyd MS (1953-59); index TS (1983)
MELTON, HIGH Ch & Chyd TS (1983)
MELTON, WEST Ch & Chyd (1984)

MENSTON High Royds Hospital B.g. TS (1981)

METHLEY Ch Bloom's Yorks MSS vol 6, 162-168 (copied 1891)

MEXBROUGH Ch & Chyd TS (1983)

MIDDLESBROUGH Ayresome Gardens Cmy TS (1978)

MIDDLETON TYAS Ch & Chyd TS (1980)

MIDDLETON-ON-THE-WOLDS Chyd TS (1983)

MIRFIELD Ch *Old Yorkshire* by W. Wheater (1885) 108-110; MS (1892). Knowle Wesleyan B.g. TS (1975). Zion Baptist Chapel TS (1975). Old Nonconformist B.g. TS (1975)

MOORSHOLME Chyd TS (1983)

MORLEY St Peter Ch *The Churches of Yorkshire 1* by W. H. Hatton (1880) 66-67. St Mary in the Wood Ch extr *Misc Gen et Her* NS 3 (1880) 306-308 331-332 343-344

NEWBALD Ch *A History of South Cave* by J. G. Hall (1892) 115-117

NEWMILL Ch (? & Chyd) *The History & Topography of the Parish of Kirkburton* by H. J. Morehouse (1861) 153-154

NEWTON KYME Ch Bloom's Yorks MSS vol 7, 157-159 (copied 1892); *Top & Gen* 1 (1846) 502-504. Ch & Chyd TS (1974)

NIDD Chyd extr TS (1980)

NORMANBY Ch & Chyd TS (1983)

NORMANTON Ch Bloom's Yorks MSS vol 6, 170-173 (copied 1891); *Yorks Archaeological Journal* 5 (1879) 267-288

OSMOTHERLEY Friends B.g. TS (1975)

OWSTON Ch & Chyd TS (1981)

PATELEY BRIDGE Salem U.R.C. Bridgehousegate B.g. TS (1982)

PENISTONE Chyd MS (1911)

PONTEFRACT Chyd TS (1979). Congregational B.g. extr TS (1979)

PUDSEY Ch MS (1911). Ch & Chyd *The Churches of Yorkshire 1* by W. H. Hatton (1880) 10 17. All Saints Chap *ibid* 9; Chap & B.g. *The History of Pudsey* by S. Rayner (1887) 58-66

RASTRICK Chyd TS (1973)

RAWCLIFFE Ch Bloom's Yorks MSS vol 7, 201-202 (copied 1892)

RAWDON Ch & Chyd TS (1976)

REDCAR Ch & Chyd microfilm of TS (1960); Chyd TS (1983) copied 1953

RIPLEY Ch & Chyd TS (1983)

RIPON Ch & Chyd *A Verbatim Copy of all the Monuments, Gravestones, & Other Sepulchral Memorials in Ripon Cathedral & its Burial Ground* by Thomas Wilson (1847)

ROSSINGTON Ch & Chyd TS (1983)

ROTHERHAM Clough Road B.g. MS (1980)

ROTHWELL Ch Bloom's Yorks MSS vol 6, 175-177 (copied 1891)

ROWLEY Ch *A History of South Cave* by J. G. Hall (1892) 182-186

ROYSTON Ch *The Churches of Yorkshire 1* by W. H. Hatton (1880) 113

SADDLEWORTH Ch *The Parish Registers of St Chad, Saddleworth* by J. Radcliffe (1891) 238-239

SANDAL MAGNA Ch *The Churches of Yorkshire 1* by W. H. Hatton (1880) 78 87-89 99. Ch & Chyd extr Bloom's Yorks MSS vol 6, 178-182 183 (copied 1891)

SAXTON Ch & Chyd TS (1975)

SCAWTON Ch & Chyd TS (1969)

SCORBOROUGH Chyd TS (1981)

SCOTTON Chyd extr TS (1979). Friends B.g. TS (1975)

SELBY Ch Bloom's Yorks MSS vol 7, 142-146 (copied 1892)

SHEFFIELD St George Ch TS (1985). Wardsend Cmy TS (1984)

SHIPTON BY BENINGBROUGH Chyd TS (1969)

SIGGLESTHORNE Ch & Chyd TS (1986)

SKELBROOKE Ch & Chyd Bloom's Yorks MSS vol 7, 246-271 (copied 1892)

SKERNE Ch & Chyd TS (1982)

SNAITH Ch Bloom's Yorks MSS vol 7, 9-10 (copied 1892)

SNEATON Ch *Yorks N & Q* 5 (1909) 177-178

SOWERBY BRIDGE Chyd TS (1973)

SPOFFORTH Ch & Chyd TS (1980)

SPROTBOROUGH Ch Bloom's Yorks MSS vol 6, 115-123 (copied 1891). Ch & Chyd TS (1981)

STAINBURN Ch & Chyd TS (1977)

STAINCLIFFE Methodist B.g. TS (1975)

STAINLAND Chyd TS (1974)

STALLINGBUSK Chyd TS (1967)

STANNINGTON Ch & Chyd TS (1984). Methodist B.g. TS (1984). Underbank Unitarian B.g. TS (1980)

STRENSALL Chyd MS (1910)

SUMMERCROFT near DRAX Friends B.g. TS (1975)

SUTTON ON DERWENT Chyd TS (1970)

SWINTON Ch & Chyd TS (1985)

TADCASTER St Joseph's R.C. Ch & Chyd TS (1974)

THIRSK Friends B.g. TS (1968)

THONG, UPPER Lane Independent B.g. *History & Topography of the Parish of Kirkburton* by H. J. Morehouse (1861) 221

THORNGUMBALD Chyd TS (1981)

THORP ARCH Ch Bloom's Yorks MSS vol 7, 165-166 (copied 1892)

THRYBERGH Ch *Top* 3 (1790) 292-294
THURNSCOE Ch & Chyd TS (1985)
UPLEATHAM Ch & Chyd TS (1953). Chyd TS
(1983)
WADSLEY Chyd TS (1984)
WADWORTH Ch Bloom's Yorks MSS vol 6,
109-113 (copied 1891)
WAKEFIELD Cathedral Ch Bloom's Yorks
MSS vol 6, 12-20 (copied 1892). St John Ch
ibid 21-22 (copied 1892)
WALKINGTON Ch & Chyd TS (1986)
WARMSWORTH Ch Bloom's Yorks MSS vol
6, 94-96 (copied 1891), vol 7, 123-125 (copied
1892). Chyd TS (1977); TS (1982)
WATH UPON DEARNE Ch Bloom's Yorks
MSS vol 7, 203-204 (copied 1892)
WAWNE Ch & Chyd TS (1986)
WELTON Ch *A History of South Cave* by J. G.
Hall (1892) 226-228
WENTWORTH Ch & Chyd TS (1984)
WESTON Ch & Chyd TS (1977)
WETHERBY Ch & Chyd TS (1975).
Methodist B.g. TS (1979)
WHARRAM PERCY Chyd TS (1982)
WHELDRAKE Chyd TS (n.d.)
WHITBY Ch extr *Parish Church of St. Mary,
Whitby* by T. H. Woodwark (1923) 12-18.
Chyd Shears (1942)
WHITGIFT Ch Bloom's Yorks MSS vol. 7, 27-
28 (copied 1892)
WHITKIRK Ch *Records of the Parish of
Whitkirk* by G. W. Platt & J. W. Morkill
(1892) 34-41. Ch & Chyd TS (1979)
WIGGINGTON Chyd MS (1910)
WIGHILL Ch & Chyd TS (1980)
WITTON, EAST Chyd MS (1984)
WOOLLEY Ch *The Churches of Yorkshire 1* by
W. H. Hatton (1880) 75-76
WORSALL Chyd TS (1975)
WORSALL, HIGH Chyd TS (1977)
WORSBOROUGH Ch Bloom's Yorks MSS vol
7, 117 (copied 1892)
WRAGBY Ch & Chyd Bloom's Yorks MSS vol
7, 86-111 (copied 1892)
YARM ON TEES Ch & Chyd TS (1977)
YORK All Saints, Pavement Ch & Chyd TS
(1974). Holy Trinity, Goodramgate Ch &
Chyd *The Parish Registers of Holy Trinity,
Goodramgate 1813-1837* (Yorks FHS Pubn 4,
1980) 65-74; Chyd MS (1910). Holy Trinity,
King's Court Ch & Chyd *The Parish Registers
of Holy Trinity, King's Court* (York FHS
Pubn 2, 1979) 45-50; Chyd TS (1974). Holy
Trinity, Micklegate Ch & Chyd TS (1974).
Minster Ch *The Register of Burials in
York Minster accompanied by Monumental
Inscriptions* by Robert H. Skaife (1870)

passim; Yorks. Archaeological Journal 1
(1870) 226-330; Bloom's Yorks MSS vol 6, 34-
37 (copied 1891). St Clement Ch TS (1974). St
Crux Ch TS (1974). St Cuthbert Ch & Chyd
TS (1974). St Denys Chyd TS (1974). St
George Chyd TS (1974). St. Helen, Stonegate
Ch & Chyd TS (1974). St Lawrence Ch
Bloom's Yorks MSS vol 6, 33, vol 7, 23
(copied 1891); Ch & Chyd TS (1975). St
Margaret Ch Bloom's Yorks MSS vol 6, 33
(copied 1891); Ch & Chyd TS (1974). St
Martin, Coney Street Ch & Chyd TS (1974).
St Mary Bishophill Junior Ch & Chyd TS
(1974). St Mary Bishophill Senior Chyd TS
(1974). St Mary, Castlegate Ch & Chyd TS
(1972). St Maurice Chyd TS (1974). St
Michael le Belfry Ch Bloom's Yorks MSS vol
6, 38-42 (copied 1891). St Michael,
Spurriergate Ch & Chyd TS (1974). St Olave
Ch Bloom's Yorks MSS vol 6, 29-30 (copied
1891). St Sampson Ch TS (1974). St Saviour
Ch & Chyd TS (1976). Bar Convent B.g. TS
(1974). Bishophill Friends B.g. TS (1975).
Cholera B.g. TS (1974). Heslington Road
Friends B.g. TS (1975)

ISLE OF MAN

*Memorials of God's Acre, being Monumental
Inscriptions in the Isle of Man taken in the
Summer of 1797* by J. Feltham & E. Wright.
Manx Soc. 14 (1868). Extracts from churches
and churchyards in every parish in the Isle of
Man. Full inscriptions not given

Isle of Man Monumental Inscriptions by H.
Boddington (1914) TS. Mainly churchyards
and some churches of Cathedral of Sodor &
Man, Crosby St Lunn & St Runn, Kirk Lonan
& Old Lonan, Ballure, Ballaugh St Mary (1
only), Sulby Glen St Stephen (4 only), Peel St
Peter, Santon Sts Ann Peter & Mark, & Kirk
Arbory, Port St Mary

BALDWIN Chyd TS (c. 1985)
BALLAUGH St Mary New Church Ch & Chyd
TS (1985). St Mary Old Chyd TS (1984)
BALLURE Ch & Chyd TS (1984)
DOUGLAS Chyd extr *Manchester Genealogist*
(Summer 1974) 16-18
FOXDALE Ch & Chyd TS (1984)
KIRK ANDREAS Chyd TS (1984)
KIRK BRIDE Ch & Chyd TS (1984)
MALEW Chyd TS (1983)
MAUGHOLD Ch & Chyd TS (1985)
PEEL Cmy TS (1986)

WALES

ANGLESEY

HOLYHEAD Ch & Chyd TS (1959). Chyd extr
Manchester Genealogist 10 (Spring 1974) 16-
18 (mainly people from outside the district)
LLANDEGFAN Ch & (extr) Chyd *Cheshire
Sheaf* 3 ser xxix (1934) 38-51
LLANGWYFEN Old Ch *Memorials of the
Dead* 1 (1888) 197-200
RHOSCOLYN Ch *Cheshire Sheaf* 3 ser xxiii
(1926) 59-64

BRECON

BLACKROCK Mission Room B.g. List in
newscutting 5 Nov 1959
CLYDACH Siloam Chapel B.g. List in
newscutting 5 Nov 1959
GILWERN Chyd List in newscutting 5 Nov
1959
GLASBURY Ch & Chyd *The Registers of
Glasbury 1660-1836* by T. Wood (1904) 293-
318 320-323. Penrheol Baptist Chapel *ibid*
318-320

CARNARVON

*Gleanings from God's Acre within the Hundred
of Lleyn and Commot of Eifionydd* by J.
Jones (1903) extrs from most parishes (chs &
chyds) in Lleyn peninsula

BARDSEY ISLAND Abbey B.g. *Gwynedd
Roots* (Journal of Gwynedd F.H.S.) 2 (1982)
32-33
CONWAY Ch *Conway Parish Registers 1541-
1793* by Alice Hadley (1900). MS (1924)
CRICCIETH Ch & (extr) Chyd *Gen* 7 (1883)
161-162
LLYSFAEN MS (1924)

CARDIGAN

ABERYSTWYTH Chyd MS (1917)

CARMARTHEN

CILYCWM Ch & Chyd TS (1973); TS (1981).
New Cmy TS (1973)

LLANELLY Ch & Chyd *Llanelly Parish
Church* by A. Mee (1888) liv-lxxii
LLANFAIRARYBRYN Gosen Calvinistic
Methodist B.g. TS (1971)
YSTRADFFIN St Barnabus Chyd TS (1970).
St Paulinus Chyd TS (1970). Seion Baptist
B.g. TS (1971)

DENBIGH

DENBIGH see WHITCHURCH
DERWEN MS (n.d.)
HENLLAN Ch *Bye-gones* (1880-81) 254-255.
TS (1942)
LLANARMON IN YALE TS (1942)
LLANBEDR Old Chyd MS (n.d.)
LLANFAIR DYFFRYN CLWYD Ch MS
(n.d.); *Cheshire Sheaf* 3 ser x (1913) 63-64
LLANFAIR TALHAIARN Ch & Chyd extr
MS (n.d.)
LLANGEDWYN Ch & Chyd TS (1985)
LLANGOLLEN TS (1942)
LLANGYNHAFAL TS (1942)
LLANRHAIADR IN CINMERCH Ch & Chyd
Bye-gones (1880-81) 249-251. TS (1942)
LLANRWST Gwydir Chapel Chap *Bye-gones*
(1878-79) 106-107 120-121
LLANSANNAN Chyd TS (1974)
LLANYCHAN Ch & Chyd extr TS (1970). TS
(1942)
LLANYNYS Ch & Chyd TS of parish register
(1974). TS (1942)
NANTGLYN extr TS (1942)
PENTRE LLYN CYMMER Capel Hermon
Chap & B.g. TS (1980)
PONCIAU Mynydd Seion Congregational B.g.
TS (1984)
RHOSLLANERCHRUGOG Capel Mynydd
Seion, Ponciau Congregational B.g. TS (1984)
RUTHIN Ch MS (n.d.)
WHITCHURCH Ch *By-gones* (1880-81) 263
270-271 298-299; MS (n.d.)

FLINT

BODFARI TS (1942)
CILCAIN Ch *Cilcain and its parish church* by
F. Simpson (Flintshire Historical Society
1912) 41-46
DISERTH Ch *Bye-gones* (1880-81) 305-306
GWAUNYSCOR Ch *Bye-gones* (1880-81)
300-301
HANMER Chyd TS (1963)

NEWMARKET Ch *Newmarket Notes (Prestatyn Hundred, Flintshire)* by T. A. Glenn. Part I (1911)
RHUDDLAN Ch *Bye-gones* (1880-81) 286-287 328

GLAMORGAN

BARRY Chyd TS (1983)
CAERAU (ELY) Chyd TS (1982)
CARDIFF St John Ch & (extr) Chyd MS (1941) copied from J. H. Matthews in *Cardiff Records* 3. St Margaret, Roath Ch & (extr) Chyd MS (1941) copied from J. H. Matthews, *op. cit.* Fairoak Road Cmy MS (1940)
COGAN, OLD Chyd MS (1970); *Penarth 1841-1871* by E. A. Benjamin (1980) 154
COWBRIDGE Ch *Old Cowbridge* by L. J. Hopkin-James (1922) 154-163
EGLWYS BREWIS Chyd TS (1969)
ILSTON Ch *Pennard and West Gower* by L. Davies (1928) 55
KENFIG HILL Pisgah Welsh Baptist B.g. TS (1984)
LAVERNOCK Chyd MS (1970); *Penarth 1841-1871* by E. A. Benjamin (1980) 153
LLANDAFF Cathedral Chyd *Victorian Graves, Llandaff Cathedral* recorded by Howell's School (1984)
LLANDOUGH Ch & Chyd MS & TS (n.d.)
LLANMAES Ch & Chyd TS (1969)
LLANTWIT FARDRE Bryntirion Calvinistic Methodist B.g. TS (1984)
LLANTWIT MAJOR Ch & Chyd TS (1969). Bethel Baptist B.g. TS (1969). Bethesda'r Fro Congregational Chap & B.g. TS (1969). Ebenezer Congregational B.g. TS (1969). Tabernacle Calvinistic Methodist B.g. TS (1969)
LLYSWORNEY Ch TS (1971)
MERTHYR DYFAN Chyd TS (1983)
MERTHYR TYDFIL Chyd TS (n.d.)
MICHAELSTON SUPER ELY Chyd TS (c. 1984)
PENARTH Ch & Chyd MS (1970). Chyd *Penarth 1841-1871* by E. A. Benjamin (1980) 151-152
PENMARK Ch & Chyd TS (1984)
PENNARD Ch *Pennard and West Gower* by L. Davies (1928) 40-41
RADYR Chyd TS (c. 1955). Waterhall Chyd MS (c. 1955)
ST DONATS Chyd TS (1969)
SULLY Ch & Chyd extr TS (1943)
WENVOE Ch & Chyd TS (1944)
WHITCHURCH Chyd MS & TS (n.d.)

MERIONETH

CORWEN Ch & Chyd MS (n.d.)
LLANDDERFEL Chyd MS (n.d.)
LLANDRILLO Ch & (extr) Chyd MS (n.d.)
LLANGAR Ch & Chyd MS (n.d.). Chyd extr *Gleanings from God's Acre* by J. Jones (1903) appendix
LLANSANTFRAID GLYN DYFRDWY Chyd extr MS (n.d.)
PENRHYN DEUDRAETH Ch & Chyd extr *Gleanings from God's Acre* by J. Jones (1903) appendix

MONMOUTH

A History of Monmouthshire by J. A. Bradney, 4 vols (1904-1933) contains MI from parishes throughout the county

ABERGAVENNY Priory Church and Close (R.C. only) *Cath Rec Soc* 12 (1913) 257-259
BEDWELTY MS & TS (1960)
BETTWS Chyd TS (1942)
BISHTON Ch & Chyd TS (1985)
BLACKWOOD Jerusalem Chapel B.g. TS (1985). Libanus Baptist B.g. TS (1985)
BLAENAVON Chyd TS (1960)
BRYNGWYN (R.C. only) *Cath Rec Soc* 12 (1913) 256
BRYNITHEL (ABERTILLERY) Old Chyd TS (1946-47)
CAERLEON Baptist Chap & B.g. TS (1985)
CASTEL Y BWCH Zoar Baptist B.g. TS (1985)
CASTLETON Cmy TS (1946-47). Baptist Chap & B.g. TS (c. 1985). Methodist B.g. TS (c. 1985)
CHAPEL HILL Chyd TS (1985)
CHEPSTOW Ch & Chyd (R.C. only) *Cath Rec Soc* 12 (1913) 251. Chyd MS (1911)
CHRISTCHURCH Ch & Chyd TS (1985)
COEDKERNEW Ch & Chyd TS (c. 1985)
CWMCARN Nazareth Baptist B.g. TS (1985)
CWMCARVAN Chyd (R.C. only) *Cath Rec Soc* 12 (1913) 247
CWMFELLINFACH Babel B.g. TS (1985)
DINGESTOW Ch & Chyd (R.C. only) *Cath Rec Soc* 12 (1913) 245-246
DIXTON Chyd (R.C. only) *Cath Rec Soc* 12 (1913) 239
GOLDCLIFF Ch & Chyd TS (1942); TS (c. 1985). Chyd TS (1946-47)
HENLLYS Ch & Chyd TS (1953); TS (1980); TS (1984). Chyd TS (1942)
KEMEYS INFERIOR Chyd TS (1984)
LANGSTONE Ch & Chyd TS (1985)

LLANARTH Ch & Chyd (R.C. only) *Cath Rec
Soc* 12 (1913) 252-256
LLANBADOC Chyd TS (1985)
LLANDENNY Chyd (R.C. only) *Cath Rec Soc*
12 (1913) 249-250
LLANDEVAND Ch & Chyd TS (1985)
LLANFAIR CILGOED Chyd (R.C. only) *Cath
Rec Soc* 12 (1913) 243-244
LLANFAIR KILGEDDIN Ch & Chyd TS
(1986)
LLANFIHANGEL LLANTARNAM Ch &
Chyd TS (c. 1985)
LLANFIHANGEL ROGGIETT Ch & Chyd TS
(1985)
LLANFIHANGEL YSTERN LLEWERN Ch
& (extr) Chyd *Misc Gen et Her* 2 ser iii (1890)
284 294-296
LLANGATTOCK VIBON AVEL Chyd (R.C.
only) *Cath Rec Soc* 12 (1913) 239-240
LLANGIBBY Ch & Chyd TS (1985). Bethel
Baptist B.g. TS (1986)
LLANGOVEN Ch (R.C. only) *Cath Rec Soc* 12
(1913) 250
LLANHENNOCK Ch & Chyd TS (1985)
LLANLLOWELL Ch & Chyd TS (1985)
LLANMARTIN Ch & Chyd TS (1986). Bethel
Presbyterian B.g. TS (1986)
LLANTILIO CROSSENY Ch & Chyd (R.C.
only) *Cath Rec Soc* 12 (1913) 241-243. See
also LLANFAIR CILGOED
LLANTRISANT Ch & Chyd TS (1985)
LLANVACHES Ch & Chyd TS (1985).
Bethany Baptist B.g. (1985). Tabernacle
United Reform Chap & B.g. TS (1985)
LLANWERN Ch & Chyd TS (1985). Chyd extr
MS (c. 1956)
MALPAS Ch & Chyd TS (1984)
MARSHFIELD Ch & Chyd TS (1985)
MICHAELSTONE Y FEDW Ch & Chyd TS
(1985). Tirzah Baptist B.g. TS (c. 1985)
MITCHEL TROY Ch & Chyd (R.C. only) *Cath
Rec Soc* 12 (1913) 238-239
MONMOUTH Chyd (R.C. only) *Cath Rec Soc*
12 (1913) 234-235
NASH Ch & Chyd TS (1942); TS (c. 1985).
Baptist Chap & B.g. TS (1984); B.g. extr TS
(1942)
NEWPORT St Woollos Ch & Chyd TS (1984);
(R.C. only) *Cath Rec Soc* 12 (1913) 259-262.
Charles Street Baptist Chap & B.g. TS (1986).
Commercial Street Baptist B.g. TS (1984).
Ebenezer Chap & B.g. TS (1984). Mount Zion
Congregational B.g. TS (1986)
PENHOW Ch & Chyd TS (1985)
PENYCLAWDD Chyd (R.C. only) *Cath Rec
Soc* 12 (1913) 247
PETERSTONE Ch TS (c. 1985)

REDWICK Ch & Chyd TS (1984)
RISCA Bethesda Baptist Chap & B.g. TS
(1986). Old Moriah Baptist B.g. TS (c. 1985)
ROCKFIELD Chyd (R.C. only) *Cath Rec Soc*
12 (1913) 235-236
ROGERSTONE Chyd TS (1942)
RUMNEY Ch & Chyd TS (1940)
ST BRIDES NETHERWENT Ch & Chyd TS
(1985); Chyd MS (1958)
ST BRIDES WENTLLOOG Ch & Chyd TS (c.
1985). Providence Congregational B.g. TS (c.
1985). Rehoboth B.g. TS (c. 1985)
ST MAUGHANS Ch & Chyd (R.C. only) *Cath
Rec Soc* 12 (1913) 240-241
ST MELLONS Ch & Chyd TS (1947)
SHIRENEWTON Ch & Chyd TS (1986)
SKENFRITH Ch & Chyd (R.C. only) *Cath Rec
Soc* 12 (1913) 244-245
TREDUNNOCK Ch & Chyd TS (c. 1985).
Chyd (R.C. only) *Cath Rec Soc* 12 (1913)
251-252
TREVETHIN Cmy MS (1959)
USK Priory Chyd (R.C. only) *Cath Rec Soc* 12
(1913) 247-249. St Francis Xavier B.g. *ibid* 249
WENTWOOD Gilgol B.g. TS (c. 1985)
WHITSON Ch & Chyd TS (1942); TS (c. 1985)
WILCRICK Ch & Chyd TS (1985)

MONTGOMERY

ABERHAFESP Ch & (extr) Chyd *Gen* NS 29
(1913) 115-117
CARNO Chyd extr *Bye-gones* (1871-73) 157
GUILSFIELD Ch & Chyd *Mont Coll* 30 (1903)
82-93
LLANYBLODWEL Ch & (extr) Chyd *Mont
Coll* 34 (1905) 55-59 62-64
MONTGOMERY Ch *Mont Coll* 46 (1940)
113-123
WELSHPOOL Ch & (extr) Chyd *Mont Coll* 15
(1882) 292-308

PEMBROKE

AMROTH Ch TS (1969)
CAMROSE Ch & Chyd *West Wales Historical
Records* 11 (1926) 23-36
CAREW CHERITON Ch TS (1969)
FISHGUARD Chyd TS (1970) burials 1756-
1799 only
GUMFRESTON Ch TS (1969)
LUDCHURCH Ch TS (1969)
NARBERTH Ch TS (1969)
PENALLY Ch TS (1969)

RHOSCROWTHER Ch *Memorials of the
Dead* 1 (1888) 100-103
RUDBAXTON Ch & Chyd *West Wales
Historical Records* 10 (1924) 24-42
ST DAVIDS Cathedral & Chyd MS (n.d.)
ST FLORENCE Ch TS (1969)
TENBY Ch extr TS (1969)

RADNOR

BETTWS DISSERTH Ch TS (1982)
CASCOB Chyd MS (1914)
CEFNLLYS Caebach Independent Chap & B.g.
TS (1983)
CREGINA Ch & Chyd TS (1983)
LLANANNO Ch & Chyd TS (1981) copied c.
1905
LLANBADARN FYNYDD Chyd TS (1981)
copied c. 1906-07
LLANBADARN Y GARREG Ch & Chyd TS
(1982)
LLANBISTER Ch TS (1981) copied c. 1905
LLANFAREDD Ch & Chyd TS (1982)
LLANSANTFFRAED IN ELVEL Chyd TS
(1982)
NANTMEL Carmel Congregational Chap &
B.g. TS (1982)
PRESTEIGNE Ch & Chyd MS (1922)
RHULEN Chyd TS (1982)
ST HARMON Chyd TS (1981) copied c. 1905

SCOTLAND

*An Theater of Mortality: Collection of Epitaphs
and Monumental Inscriptions chiefly in
Scotland* by R. Monteith (repr 1834). TS
index (n.d.) to original edition published
1704-13

*Monuments and Monumental Inscriptions in
Scotland* by C. Rogers. Vol. 1 (1871), Vol. 2
(1872). Extrs from churches and churchyards
throughout country

*Epitaphs and Inscriptions from Burial Grounds
and Old Buildings in the North East of
Scotland* by A. Jervise. Vol. 1 (1875), Vol. 2
(1879). Extrs mainly from counties of
Aberdeen, Angus, Banff, Kincardine, Moray

Inscriptions from Churchyards" by J. Jameson
(1961) MS. Alloa, Anworth, Cambuskenneth

Abbey, Clackmannan, Dollar, Tillicultry,
Tullibody (Clackmannan); Aberdour,
Burntisland, Carnock, Culross, Cupar,
Dalgety, Dunfermline, Dysart, Inverkeithing,
Saline, Torryburn (Fife); Edinburgh Dean
Cmy, Edinburgh New Calton, Leith, South
Leith (Midlothian); Abercorn,
Borrowstowness, Queensferry (West Lothian);
Kincardine on Forth, Perth, Tulliallan (Perth):
Airth, St Ninians (Stirling). Older stones only

ABERDEEN

Aberdeenshire Epitaphs and Inscriptions by J.
A. Henderson (1907). Extrs from churches and
churchyards in many parishes

The Thanage of Fermartyn by W. Temple
(1894). Includes Auchterless, Belhelvie,
Bourtie, Drumblade, Ellon, Fintray, Folla-
Rule, Forgue, Foveran, Fyvie, Kinkell,
Kinmuck, Logiebuchan, Methlic, Monkeggie,
Monycaboc, New Machar, Tarves, Udny,
Woodhead

*Pre-1855 Gravestone Inscriptions in Upper
Deeside* by A. G. & M. H. Beattie (1985) TS.
Covers Aboyne and Glentanar, Birse, Coull,
Crathie and Braemar, Glenmuick, Tullich and
Glengairn, Kincardine O'Neil, Logie-
Coldstone, Lumphanan, Tarland

ABERDEEN St Andrew Ch *Aberdeen Journal,
Notes & Queries* 3 (1910) 34-36 40-42 90-91
105-106 111-112 272-273. St Clement Ch *ibid* 1
(1908) 142. St John Ch *ibid* 2 (1909) 288-290
298-299. St Nicholas Ch & Chyd *Scottish
Notes & Queries* 1 ser i (1887-88) *passim;* ii
(1888-89) *passim;* iii (1889-90) *passim;* vii
(1893-94) 4-5; viii (1894-95) *passim;* ix
(1895-96) 97-98 151-152; index of names in
general index to first series. St Paul Ch
Aberdeen Journal, Notes & Queries 2 (1909)
302-304. St Peter Ch & Chyd (Moir family)
ibid 3 (1910) 203-204 257-258. Allenvale Cmy
South microfilm of MS (n.d.). John Knox
Chyd TS (c. 1985). Bay of Nigg, St Fittick
Chyd TS (1970)
BELHELVIE Chyd TS (1984)
BOURTIE Chyd TS (1986)
CHAPEL OF GARIOCH Chyd & Logie-
Durno Chyd TS (1986)
DUNBENNAN Chyd *Moray* ii 397-404
FETTERNEAR St John Chyd extr & St Ninian
Chyd extr *Aberdeen & North-East Scotland
F.H.S. Newsletter* 16 (Sept 1985) 14-15
FINTRAY Hatton Chyd TS (1985)

FYVIE Millbrex Chyd & Woodhead Episcopal Chyd TS (1984)
GARTLEY Chyd *Moray* ii 417-420
GILCOMSTON Ch *Aberdeen Journal, Notes & Queries* 2 (1909) 195-196
HUNTLY see DUNBENNAN and KINNOIR
KEITH-HALL & KINKELL Chyds TS (1984)
KING-EDWARD Old Chyd TS (1982)
KINNOIR Chyd *Moray* ii 406-411
LESLIE Chyd TS (1983)
MELDRUM, OLD Episcopal Chyd TS (1986)
MONYMUSK Chyd TS (1986)
PEATHILL (OLD PITSLIGO) Old Chyd TS (1984)
RHYNIE Chyd TS (1984)

ANGUS

Pre-1855 Gravestone Inscriptions in Angus by A. Mitchell (ed.). Vol. 1 Strathmore (1979) TS. Vol. 2 Seacoast (1981) TS. Vol. 3 Environs of Dundee (1983) TS. Vol. 4 Dundee & Broughty Ferry (1984) TS. Includes all parishes

ARBILOT Ch & Chyd TS (1958)
ARBROATH Abbey Chyd extr MS & TS (1961)
BARRY Chyd TS (1953)
BENVIE Chyd microfilm of MS (1951)
BRECHIN Cathedral B.g. extr MS (1961)
DUNDEE St Andrew Chyd microfilm of MS (n.d.). St Peter Chyd microfilm of MS (n.d.). Howff B.g. *History of Dundee* by J. MacLaren (1874) 393-419; microfilm of MS (n.d.). Old South Ch MacLaren, *op. cit.* 211-215. Balgay Cmy MS (n.d.). Bell Street Cmy TS (1960). Logie (Lochee) Chyd TS (1951); microfilm of MS (n.d.). Roodyard Cmy microfilm of MS (n.d.). Eastern Necropolis, Arbroath Road Jewish TS (n.d.). Broughty Ferry see MONIFIETH
FOWLIS Chyd microfilm of MS (1951)
INVERARITY Chyd MS (1953)
INVERGOWRIE Dargie Ch & Chyd TS & MS (1951)
KETTINS Chyd TS (1953)
LIFF Chyd microfilm of MS (n.d.)
LUNDIE Chyd MS (1952)
MAINS Chyd microfilm of MS (n.d.). Old Mains Chyd microfilm of MS (n.d.)
MONIFIETH Ch & Chyd TS (n.d.). Broughty Ferry Chyd microfilm of MS (n.d.); Old B.g. between tenements TS (1953)
MURROES Chyd MS (n.d.)
ST VIGEANS Ch & Chyd TS (1958)

STRATHMARTINE Cmy microfilm of MS (n.d.)
TEALING Chyd MS (n.d.)

ARGYLL

LISMORE & APPIN Isla Munda Burial Isle TS (1969)
OBAN Old Chyd microfilm of TS (n.d.)

AYR

Pre-1855 Gravestone Inscriptions in Kilmarnock and Loudoun District by A. G. & M. H. Beattie (1985) TS. Includes parishes of Dunlop, Fenwick, Galston, Kilmarnock, Kilmaurs, Loudoun, Riccarton, Stewarton

Cumnock and Doon Valley Graveyard Inscriptions (Manpower Services Commission, 1986) 3 vols, TS. Covers Auchinleck, Catrine, Cumnock, Dalmellington, Dalrymple, Mauchline, Muirkirk, New Cumnock, Ochiltree, Patna, Sorn, Stair

ALLOA Greenside Cmy MS (n.d.)
AYR Old Chyd TS (1974). Moravian Chyd *Scottish Notes & Queries* 3 ser xi (1933) 133-136
DUNLOP Chyd extr *Archaeological and Historical Collections of Ayr and Wigton* 4 (1884) 41-46
KILBIRNIE Chyd extr *Archaeological and Historical Collections of Ayr and Wigton* 2 (1880) 128-135
KILMARNOCK Chyd microfilm of TS & MS (n.d.)
LOUDOUN Newmilns Old Cmy extr MS (n.d.)

BANFF

The Chronicles of Keith by J. F. S. Gordon (1880). Includes Botriphnie, Cairnie, Drumdelgy, Grange, Keith, Ruthven

Pre-1855 Gravestone Inscriptions on Speyside by A. Mitchell (1970-74) TS. Includes B.gs. in parishes of Aberlour and Inveraven

ABERLOUR Chyd *Moray* i 182-186
ALVAH Old Chyd TS (1983)
FORGLEN Chyd TS (1983)
GAMRIE Chyd extr *Aberdeen Journal, Notes & Queries* 1 (1908) 42-43

INVERAVON Chyd *Moray* i 209-214
INVERKEITHNY Chyd TS (1983)
KIRKMICHAEL Chyd *Moray* i 221-224
MARNOCH Chyd *Moray* ii 391-396
MORTLACH Ch & Chyd *Moray* i 146-155

BERWICK

The Churches and Churchyards of Berwickshire
by J. Robson (1896). Extrs from all parishes
except Hume

*Pre-1855 Tombstone Inscriptions in
Berwickshire* by D. C. Cargill (1967-70) TS.
Covers all parishes

BUNKLE & PRESTON Chyds (pre-1825) *The
Session Book of Bunkle and Preston 1665-
1690* by J. Hardy (1900) lvii-lxxix

CLACKMANNAN

*Monumental Inscriptions (pre-1855) in
Clackmannanshire* by J. F. & S. Mitchell
(1968) TS. Covers all parishes including Alva
(Stirling)

DUMFRIES

APPLEGARTH & SIBBALDBIE Applegarth
Chyd TS (1972). Sibbaldbie Chyd TS (1967)
BRYDEKIRK Chyd TS (1963)
CAERLAVEROCK Ch & Chyd TS (1968)
CORRIE Chyd TS (1968)
CUMMERTREES Chyd TS (1965).
Repentance Tower B.g. TS (1964)
DALTON Chyd TS (1965). Little Dalton Chyd
offprint from *Transactions of the
Dumfriesshire and Galloway Natural History
and Antiquarian Society* 33 (1954-55); TS
(1965)
DORNOCK Chyd TS (1964)
DRYFESDALE Old Dryfe Chyd & Lockerbie
Chyd TS (1967)
DUMFRIES St Michael Ch & Chyd *Memorials
of St. Michael's, the Old Parish Church of
Dumfries* by W. M'Dowall (1876)
ESKDALEMUIR Chyd TS (1970). Watcarrick
Chyd TS (1970)
GRAITNEY (GRETNA) Chyd TS (1965)
HALF-MORTON Chyd & Morton Tower of
Sark B.g. TS (1965)
HODDAM Chyd, Ecclefechan Chyd, Luce B.g.,
St Kentigern B.g. TS (1965)

HUTTON Chyd TS (1968)
JOHNSTONE Chyd TS (1966)
KEIR, OLD Chyd extr offprint from
*Transactions of the Dumfriesshire and
Galloway Natural History and Antiquarian
Society* 32 (1953-54)
KIRKCONNEL Chyd TS (1966)
KIRKMICHAEL Garrell Chyd TS (1968)
KIRKPATRICK-FLEMING Chyd TS (1964)
KIRKPATRICK-JUXTA Chyd TS (1972)
LANGHOLM Old Chyd TS (1969). Wauchope
Chyd TS (1968). Staplegordon Chyd TS
(1971)
LOCHMABEN Chyd TS (1967)
MIDDLEBIE, PENNERSAUGHS &
CARRUTHERS Chyds TS (1965)
MOFFAT Chyd TS (1971)
MOUSWALD Chyd TS (1967)
RUTHWELL Chyd TS (1966)
ST MUNGO Chyd TS (1966)
TINWALD Trailflatt Chyd TS (1971)
TORTHORWALD Chyd TS (1968)
TUNDERGARTH Chyd TS (1966)
WAMPHRAY Chyd TS (1968)
WESTERKIRK Chyd TS (1970)

DUNBARTON

*Monumental Inscriptions (pre-1855) in
Dunbartonshire* by J. F. & S. Mitchell (1969)
TS. All known and accessible burial grounds.
Some MI later than 1855

FIFE

Monumental Inscriptions (pre-1855) in East Fife
by J. F. & S. Mitchell (1971) TS. *Monumental
Inscriptions (pre-1855) in West Fife* by J. F. &
S. Mitchell (1972) TS. All known and
accessible burial grounds. Includes Culross
and Tulliallan (previously Perthshire)

PITTENWEEM Chyd microfilm of MS (n.d.)

INVERNESS

Pre-1855 Gravestone Inscriptions on Speyside
by A. Mitchell (1970-74) TS. Includes B.gs. in
parishes of Abernethy, Alvie, Cromdale,
Inverallan & Advie, Garten & Kincardine,
Insh, Kingussie, Laggan, Rothiemurchus

CLUNY B.g. *Scottish Genealogist* 15:4 (1968)
73-80

CROMDALE Chyd *Moray* i 236-238
GLENELG Old & New B.gs. TS (1985)
KILLMALLIE B.gs. *Pre-1855 Gravestone
Inscriptions in Lochaber* by L. & R. Tatler
(1980) TS
KILMONIVAIG B.gs. Tatler, *op. cit.*

KINCARDINE

BANCHORY-DEVENICK Ch & Chyd *History
of the Parish of Banchory-Devenick* by J. A.
Henderson (1890) 274 297-319
DUNNOTTAR Chyd (Old Section) TS (1985)
KINNEFF Ch (Honyman family) *Aberdeen
Journal, Notes & Queries* 2 (1909) 284-285
NIGG Ch *Aberdeen Journal, Notes & Queries* 1
(1908) 87-88
STRACHAN Chyd TS (1984)

KINROSS

Monumental Inscriptions in Kinross-shire by J.
F. & S. Mitchell (1967) TS. All visible
inscriptions in the county's eleven old burial
grounds

KIRKCUDBRIGHT

GIRTHON Old Chyd *Dumfriesshire and
Galloway Natural History and Antiquarian
Society: Record Text Publications* 1 (1980)
1-32
LOCKRUTTON Chyd TS (1974)

LANARK

*Monumental Inscriptions (pre-1855) in the
Upper Ward of Lanarkshire* by S. A. Scott
(1977) TS. All known and accessible burial
grounds
AIRDRIE New Monkland Cmy extr microfilm
of MS (n.d.)
GLASGOW Anderston, Heddle Place Old Chyd
extr MS (1956). Anderston, St Mark,
Cheapside Street Chyd extr MS (1956). North
Street Cmy MS (1956). St David (Ramshorn)
Ch & Old & New Chyds TS (1983); extr MS
(1956)
GOVAN Chyd MS (1956)

MIDLOTHIAN

COLINTON St Cuthbert Chyd MS (1969)
EDINBURGH Greyfriars Old & New Ch &
Chyd *The Epitaphs and Monumental
Inscriptions in Greyfriars Churchyard,
Edinburgh* by J. Brown (1867); Chyd
microfilm of MS (1958). Holyrood Abbey Ch
offprint from *The Chapel Royal of
Holyroodhouse* n.a. (n.d.) 44-60. St Cuthbert
Chyd "Monumental Inscriptions in St
Cuthbert's Churchyard. Edinburgh" by J.
Smith in *Scottish Record Society* 47 (1915) &
51 (1919). St John the Evangelist Ch & extr
Chyd *Memorials of the Church of St John the
Evangelist, Princes Street, Edinburgh* by G. F.
Terry (1911). St Mary Cathedral, Palmerston
Place Ch extr MS (1960). Old Calton Cmy,
Waterloo Place *Scottish Genealogist* 3:2 (1956)
33-34. Buccleuch Chyd MS (1974). East
Preston Street Cmy MS (1959). Greendykes
Chyd extr TS (1974). Portobello Old Chyd
MS (1967). Restalrig Chyd MS (1908). Old
Jewish Cmy, Braid Place extr TS (1949).
Newington Jewish Cmy MS (1951)
INVERESK Musselburgh St Michael Ch &
Chyd MS (n.d.)
LEITH, NORTH Madeira Street Ch MS
(1960). Coburg Street Chyd MS (1960);
Scottish Genealogist 3:3 (1956) 58-64
LEITH, SOUTH Kirkgate Ch & Chyd TS (n.d.)
MID-CALDER Chyd extr *The Parish of Mid-
Calder* by H. B. M'Call (1894) 211-212

WEST LOTHIAN

*Monumental Inscriptions (pre-1855) in West
Lothian* by J. F. & S. Mitchell (1969) TS. All
known and accessible burial grounds

MORAY

Pre-1855 Gravestone Inscriptions on Speyside
by A. Mitchell (1970-74) TS. Includes B.gs. in
parishes of Bellie, Knockando, Rothes,
Speymouth

ALVES Chyd *Moray* ii 150-152
BELLIE Chyd *Moray* i 61-65
BIRNIE Chyd *Moray* ii 44-46
DALLAS Chyd *Moray* ii 51-53
DUTHIL Chyd *Moray* i 255-259
DYKE Ch & Chyd *Moray* ii 236-241
ELCHIES Chyd *Moray* i 115-116

ELGIN Cathedral Ch & Chyd *Moray* i 59-61
387-404. Greyfriars Ch *ibid.* 405
KINNEDAR Chyd *Moray* ii 72-73
KNOCKANDO Chyd *Moray* i 116-119
LHANBRYDE ST ANDREWS Chyd *Moray* i
341-346
MOY Chyd *Moray* ii 205-207
OGSTON Chyd *Moray* ii 76-77
SPEYMOUTH Chyd *Moray* i 310-312
SPYNIE Chyd *Moray* ii 139-145
URQUHART Chyd *Moray* i 324-326

PEEBLES

*Monumental Inscriptions (pre-1855) in
Peeblesshire* by S. A. Scott (1971) TS. All
known and accessible burial grounds

PEEBLES Chyd extr *N & Q* 173 (1937) 458
WEST LINTON Chyd MS (1962)

PERTH

*Monumental Inscriptions (pre-1855) in South
Perthshire* by J. F. & S. Mitchell (1974) TS.
*Monumental Inscriptions (pre-1855) in North
Perthshire* by J. F. & S. Mitchell (1975) TS.
Cover every parish

BALQUHIDDER Chyd MS (1961)
CULROSS see county of FIFE
MEIGLE Chyd TS (1972)
TULLIALLAN see county of FIFE

RENFREW

*Monumental Inscriptions (pre-1855) in
Renfrewshire* by J. F. & S. Mitchell (1969) TS.
All known and accessible burial grounds

EAGLESHAM Chyd MS (n.d.)
GOUROCK B.g. extr *Scottish Genealogist* 17:4
(1970) 117-119
PAISLEY New Street B.g. extr MS (1956)
PORT GLASGOW Campbell Street B.g.
Scottish Genealogist 6:2 (1959) 7-8

ROSS

GAIRLOCH Annat New B.g. TS (1985)
KINLOCHLUICHART Chyd TS (1985)
LOCHCARRON Chyd TS (1985). Kishorn B.g.
TS (1984)
TAIN St Duthus Ch & Chyd MS (1972)

ROXBURGH

ASHKIRK see county of SELKIRK
CANONBIE Chyd TS (1969)
CASTLETON Chyd & Hermitage Chapel TS
(1972). Ettletoun Chyd TS (1971)
EWES Chyd TS (1968). Unthank Chyd TS
(1968)

SELKIRK

ASHKIRK Chyd TS (1961). Lindean Chyd TS
(1961)
GALASHIELS Old Chyd TS (1962); MS (n.d.).
Bewlie B.g. TS (1962). Ladhope B.g. TS
(1962); MS (1973). St Peter Episcopal Chyd
MS (1973). For LINDEAN see ASHKIRK
SELKIRK Old Chyd TS (1961)

SHETLAND

FAIR ISLE Chyd MS (1973)

STIRLING

*Monumental Inscriptions (pre-1855) in East
Stirlingshire* by J. F. & S. Mitchell (1972) TS.
*Monumental Inscriptions (pre-1855) in West
Stirlingshire* by J. F. & S. Mitchell (1973) TS.
All known and accessible burial grounds (for
Alva see county of Clackmannan)

SUTHERLAND

CREICH Chyd MS (1972)

IRELAND

*Journal of the Association for the Preservation
of the Memorials of the Dead in Ireland* 2-10
(1892-1920), continued as *Journal of the Irish
Memorials Association* 11-13 (1921-1937).
Many MIs from churches and churchyards
throughout Ireland. *An Index of the
Churchyards and Buildings in the Journal of
the APMDI 1888-1908* (1909) lists the places
covered up to 1908

"Some Irish Monumental Inscriptions in England" by H. E. Jones in *Irish Ancestor* 1:2 (1969) 97-103

"Monuments of Irish Interest in St Isidore's, Rome" by G. Mott in *Irish Ancestor* 10:1 (1978) 15-17

"Tombstones of Some Irish Emigrants in the Catholic Cemetery at Andover, Massachusetts" by P. M. Doherty in *Irish Ancestor* 4:1 (1972) 23-26

"Some Irish Inscriptions in Old Burial Grounds of New South Wales, Australia" by K. A. Johnson in *Irish Ancestor* 3:1 (1971) 5-10 (Liverpool, Penrith, Gegedzerick); 5:2 (1973) 76-83 (Sydney — Sandhills Cmy)

CO. ANTRIM

BALLYCLARE Chyd microfilm of MS (1958)
BELFAST Christ Church Ch *Gravestone Inscriptions. Belfast* 1 by R. S. J. Clarke (1982). St George Ch *ibid*. Charitable Institution B.g. microfilm of TS (n.d.). Friar's Bush B.g. *Gravestone Inscriptions. Belfast* 2 by T. Merrick (1984). Milltown Cmy *ibid*. Shankhill B.g. R.S.J. Clarke, *op. cit.*
BUN-NA-MARGY Chyd MS (1911)
CULFEIGHTRIN Chyd *IA* 2:2 (1970) 131-136
DERRIAGHY Chyd *Christchurch, Derriaghy. Gravestone Inscriptions* by W. N. C. Barr & W. C. Kerr (1980)
GLYNN Ch & Chyd *Gravestone Inscriptions. County Antrim* 2 by G. Rutherford (1981)
ISLANDMAGEE Chyds G. Rutherford, *op. cit.* 1 (1977)
KILROOT Chyd G. Rutherford, *op. cit.* 2 (1981)
LAMBEG Chyd *Lambeg Churchyard, Lisburn, county Antrim. Inscriptions on old Tombstones (1626-1837) and those of special interest to present day* by W. Cassidy (1937)
MAGHERAGALL Chyd *FL* 1:2 (1981) 31-32; 1:3 (1981) 26-32
RALOO Chyds G. Rutherford, *op. cit.* 2 (1981)
TEMPLECORRAN Chyds G. Rutherford, *op. cit.* 2 (1981)

CO. CORK

KINSALE Ch *St Multose Church, Kinsale* by J. L. Darling (1895) 29-41
MOLOGGA Chyd *IG* 2:12 (1955) 390-393
YOUGHAL Ch *Top & Gen* 2 (1853) 194-207

CO. DONEGAL

BALLYSHANNON Chyd *FL* 1:3 (1981) 13-14; 1:4 (1982) 31-34

CO. DOWN

Gravestone Inscriptions. County Down 1-19 by R. S. J. Clarke (c. 1966-1983). Volumes cover Aghlisnafin 9, Annahilt 18, Ardglass 8, Ardkeen 13, Ardquin 13, Baileysmill 2, Ballee 8, Balligan 14, Balloo 17, Ballooly 19, Ballyblack 12, Ballycarn 3, Ballycopeland 16, Ballycranbeg 13, Ballycruttle 8, Ballyculter 8, Ballygalget 13, Ballygowan 5, Ballyhalbert 15, Ballyhemlin 14, Ballykinler 9, Ballymacashen 6, Ballymageogh 10, Ballymartin 10, Ballynahinch 9, Ballyphilip 13, Ballytrustan 13, Bangor 17, Blaris 5, Boardmills 2, Breda 1 13, Bright 8, Cargacreevy 18, Carrowdore 14, Carryduff 1 18, Castlereagh 1 18, Clandeboye 17, Cloghy 14, Clough 9, Comber 5 13, Copeland Island 16, Donaghadee 16, Donaghcloney 19, Downpatrick 7, Dromara 19, Dromore 19, Drumaroad 9, Drumbeg 3 6, Drumbo 1 4 5 18, Drumlough 19, Dundonald 2, Dunsfort 8, Edenderry 3, Eglantine 18, Finnis 19, Garvaghy 19, Gilnahirk 18, Glasdrumman 10, Glastry 15, Gransha 1, Grey Abbey 12, Groomsport 17, Hillhall 1, Hillsborough 18, Holywood 4 5, Inch 7, Inishargy 14, Kilcarn 5, Kilclief 8, Kilhorne 10, Kilkeel 10, Kilkinamurry 19, Killaney 2, Killaresy 6, Killinakin 6, Killinchy 5 6, Killough 8, Killybawn 1 2, Killyleagh 6 7, Killysuggan 5, Kilmegan 9, Kilmood 5, Kilmore 3 13, Kilwarlin 18, Kircubbin 12, Knock 4 13, Knockbrecken 1 18, Knockbreda 2, Legacurry 2, Lisbane 13, Loughaghery 18, Loughinisland 9 12, Lurganville 18, Magheradrool 9 12, Magherahamlet 9, Magheralin 19, Maze 18, Millisle 16, Moira 18, Moneyrea 1, Mourne 10, Movilla 11, Newtownards 11, Old Court 8, Portaferry 13, Rademan 3, Raffrey 5, Rathmullan 9, Ravara 5, Rossglass 8, Saintfield 3, Saul 7 8, Seaforde 9, Slanes 14, Tamlaght 10, Templepatrick 14, Tullymacnous 6, Tullynakill 1 3 5, Waringstown 19, Whitechurch 15

COPELAND ISLAND Cmy microfilm of MS (n.d.)
DONAGHCLONEY, OLD Chyd *An Ulster Parish: being a History of Donaghcloney (Waringstown)* by E. D. Atkinson (1898) 125-129

LISBURN Cathedral Chyd microfilm of MS
(n.d.)
WARINGSTOWN Ch & Chyd E. D. Atkinson,
op. cit. 120-125

CO. DUBLIN

ABBOTSTOWN B.g. *IG* 6:6 (1985) 824-827
BLACKROCK Dean's Grange Cmy microfilm
of TS (n.d.)
CHAPELIZOD Ch & Chyd *IG* 5:4 (1977)
496-505
CLONSILLA Chyd *IG* 6:5 (1984) 680-684
DALKEY Ch & Chyd *IG* 5:2 (1975) 250-254
DUBLIN Christ Church Cathedral Ch *Some
Irish Lists* 6 by G. S. Cary, TS (1947) 90-119.
St Andrew coffin plates *IG* 5:1 (1974) 131-139.
St Michael & St John coffin plates *IG* 5:3
(1976) 368-369. Ballybough Jewish Cmy *The
Jews of Ireland* by L. Hyman (1972) 267-272
ESKER Chyd *IG* 6:1 (1980) 54-58
GLASNEVIN Prospect Cmy extr *Louisiana
Genealogical Register* 22:3 (Sept 1975) 265-275
KILBRIDE Chyd *IG* 6:3 (1982) 378-380
KILLINEY Old Chyd *IG* 4:6 (1973) 647-648
KILMACTALWAY Chyd *IG* 6:3 (1982) 380
KILMAHUDDRICK Chyd *IG* 6:3 (1982) 381
LEIXLIP Chyd *IG* 4:2 (1969) 110-116
LOUGHTOWN LOWER Chyd *IG* 6:3 (1982)
380-381
LUCAN Ch & Chyd *IG* 5:6 (1979) 763-767
MONKSTOWN Ch *St John's, Monkstown* by
R. W. Harden (1911) 68-69 87. Chyd *IG* 4:3
(1970) 201-212; 4:4 (1971) 349-362
NEWCASTLE Ch & Chyd *IG* 6:2 (1981)
219-226
PALMERSTOWN Ch & Chyd *IG* 5:5 (1978)
650-653
RATHCOOLE Ch & Chyd *IG* 6:4 (1983)
523-525
TANEY Ch & Chyd *The Parish of Taney. A
History of Dundrum, near Dublin, and its
Neighbourhood* by F. E. Ball & E. Hamilton
(1895) 27-52 63-64

CO. FERMANAGH

ENNISKILLEN Ch & Chyd *Enniskillen Parish
and Town* by W. H. Dundas (1913) 42-44
91-119

CO. GALWAY

KILMACDUAGH Ch & Chyd *IA* 7:1 (1975)
26-35

CO. KERRY

KILLARNEY Ch & Chyd *Misc Gen et Her*
2 ser iv (1892) 60-61

CO. KILKENNY

KILBRIDE B.g. *IA* 18:1 (1986) 37-47

CO. LIMERICK

ARDCANNY *IA* 9:1 (1977) 3-5
GRANGE Chyd *IA* 10:1 (1980) 49-51
KILBEHENNY Chyd *IG* 2:11 (1954) 349-354
NANTINAN Chyd *IA* 12:1 & 2 (1980) 53-62
RATHKEALE Chyd *IA* 14:2 (1982) 105-120;
16:1 (1984) 53

CO. LONDONDERRY

AGHANLOO New Ch & (extr) Old Chyd
Historical Gleanings from County Derry by S.
Martin (n.d.) 42-45. Old Chyd & Church of
Ireland Chyd *FL* 2:3 (1985) 15-16
BALLYKELLY Chyd B.g. ½ mile north of
village, Presbyterian B.g., R.C. B.g. *FL* 2:3
(1985) 16-19; 2:4 (1985) 12-19
BALTEAGH Chyd & Presbyterian B.g. *FL* 2:4
(1985) 20-21
CAMUS JUXTA BANN Chyd *Scottish
Genealogist* 11:2 (1964) 6-28
DRUMACHOSE Old Chyd & Presbyterian
B.g. *FL* 2:4 (1985) 21-22; 2:5 (1985) 19-20
EDENDERRY Ch *The Parish of Edenderry* by
H. I. Law (1949) 23-27
LARGY Presbyterian B.g. *FL* 2:5 (1985) 20-21
LIMAVADY Presbyterian B.g. & R.C. B.g. *FL*
2:5 (1985) 21-24
MACOSQUIN see CAMUS JUXTA BANN
TAMLAGHT Chyd *FL* 2:4 (1985) 12-13

CO. LOUTH

ARDEE Chyd *IG* 3:1 (1956) 36-40
CASTLEBELLINGHAM Ch & Chyd *History*

of Kilsaran by J. B. Leslie (1908) 282-290
DROMISKIN Ch & Chyd J. B. Leslie. *op. cit.*
304-310
FOCHART Chyd *Tombstone Inscriptions in
Fochart Graveyard, county Louth* by D.
MacIomhair (c. 1969)
KILSARAN Chyd & R.C. Ch & Chyd J. B.
Leslie, *op. cit.* 291-299
MANSFIELDSTOWN Ch & Chyd J. B. Leslie,
op. cit. 311-317
STABANNON Ch & Chyd J. B. Leslie, *op. cit.*
300-304

CO. MEATH

AGHER Ch & Chyd *IA* 10:2 (1978) 129-139
ATHBOY Ch & Chyd *IA* 13:1 (1981) 52-63;
13:2 (1981) 113-124
BALSOON Chyd *IA* 8:2 (1976) 94-96
CLADY Ch & Chyd *IA* 16:1 (1984) 9-13
DRUMLARGAN Chyd *IA* 12:1 & 2 (1980)
82-83
DULEEK Chyd & Old Ch *IG* 3:12 (1967)
538-540
DUNBOYNE Ch & Chyd *IA* 11:1 (1979) 54-68;
11:2 (1979) 137-153
KELLS Chyd extr *IG* 3:11 (1966) 439-444
KILLACONNIGAN Chyd *IA* 16:2 (1984)
107-117
LOUGHCREW Ch & Chyd *IA* 9:2 (1977)
85-101
MOY Chyd *IA* 6:2 (1974) 85-96
MOYAGHER Chyd *IA* 8:1 (1976) 9-12
OLDCASTLE Chyd "Monumental Inscriptions
of Oldcastle, county Meath" by R. ffolliott &
H. E. Jones in *Riocht na Midhe* (c. 1967)
11-19
RATHMORE Ch & Chyd *IA* 7:2 (1975) 70-82

CO. TIPPERARY

KILMORE Chyd *IG* 2:10 (1953) 317-321
USKANE Chyd *IG* 3:2 (1957) 74-75

CO. TYRONE

CASTLE CAULFEILD Ch *History of St
Michael's Church, Castle Caulfeild (Parish of
Donaghmore)* by Y. A. Burges (1936) 8-10
CLOGHER Cathedral Ch & Chyd *Clogher
Cathedral Graveyard* by J. I. D. Johnston
(1972)

CO. WATERFORD

AFFANE *IG* 2:9 (1952) 285-289
CLASHMORE Chyd *IG* 2:8 (1950) 246-249
WHITECHURCH Chyd *IA* 5:1 (1973) 28-33

CO. WESTMEATH

BALLYLOUGHLOE (MOUNT TEMPLE)
Chyd *IA* 4:2 (1972) 105-112
DELVIN Chyd *IA* 14:1 (1982) 39-57

CO. WICKLOW

GLENDALOUGH Cathedral Chyd *IG* 2:3
(1945) 88-93

CHANNEL ISLANDS

JERSEY St Lawrence Chyd extr *Channel
Islands Family History Journal* 14 (Spring
1982) 174-176
see also CANADA, QUEBEC

OVERSEAS

ABU DHABI Non-Muslim Cmy TS (1977)

ADEN see INDIA general

AFGHANISTAN Kandahar & Kalat-i-Ghilzai
(military burials of 2nd Afghan War) *N & Q*
174 (1938) 239-242. See also INDIA, PUNJAB

AFRICA
African Monumental Inscriptions (1982) TS.
Basutoland — Mafeteng, Qacha' Nek, Leribe,
Quthing. Ghana — Cape Coast Castle, James
Fort Prison, Elmina. Kenya — Kericho
district, Kilifi Coastal Protectorate, Kisumu,
Mumias, Nairobi, Nakuru, Northern Frontier
Province, Ol Mukutan vicinity, Rift Valley
Region, graves on private property in various
places. Nigeria — provinces of Adamawa,
Bauchi, Benue, Bornu, Ilorin, Kabba, Kano,
Katsina, Niger, Plateau, Sardauna, Sokoto,
Zaria etc. Nyasaland — Port Herald,
Chiromo, Chikwawa, Nasawa, Kota Kota,
Mkhoma, Lilongwe, Mzimba, Old Bundawe,
Karonga, Livingstonia, Cape Maclear,
Palombe, Mlanje, Chiradzulu, Neno, Dedza,
Matope, Nchen, Dowa, Likoma. Sierra Leone
— Freetown. Uganda — Entebbe, Hoima,
Tororo, Jinja
ALGERIA Algiers, Holy Trinity extr *Gibraltar
Diocesan Gazette* 2:5 (Feb 1914) 92
GOLD COAST Accra, James Fort *N & Q*
12 ser x (1922) 245-246
KENYA Mumias B.g. TS (1974)
MALAWI various TS (1980)
Blantyre Presbyterian Cmy TS (1981)
MOZAMBIQUE Lourenco Marques, Old Cmy
Misc Gen et Her 4 ser ii (1908) 257
NIGERIA Kano TS (1978)
Lagos TS (1978)
Sokoto & Maiduguri TS (1978)
SIERRA LEONE Freetown, St George
Cathedral *Sierra Leone Studies* 9 (Aug 1927)
36-45
SOUTH AFRICA Cape Town, Anglican Cmy
& Dutch East India Co Cmy *Gen Mag* 10
(1950) 490-493; 11 (1951) 11-19. Anglican Cmy
(1905) Snell vol. 16, 225-229
Kuruman (Cape Province) Cmy TS (1972)
Port Elizabeth, St George Park Cmy TS (1986)
Utrecht (Natal) Cmy MS (c. 1977)
SUDAN Khartoum, Military Cmy TS (1982)

ASCENSION ISLAND St Mary Ch TS (n.d.)

AUSTRALIA
NEW SOUTH WALES Ashfield, St John
MIAu 1
Enfield, St Thomas *MIAu* 1
Kurrajong, Presbyterian Cmy TS (c. 1951)
La Perouse *MIAu* 3
Liverpool TS (c. 1937)
Mayfield, St Andrew Cmy TS (c. 1951)
Narrandera *MIAu* 2
Newcastle, Cathedral Cmy TS (c. 1951)
Newtown *MIAu* 2
Parramatta, St John Cmy MS (c. 1951); TS
(1964). Methodist Cmy TS (c. 1951)
Point Gellibrand B.g. TS (1899)
Randwick, St Jude *MIAu* 3
Ryde, St Anne's Cmy TS (1948)
Sutton Forest, All Saints Ch & Chyd TS (1957)
Sydney Cathedral *N & Q* 12 ser iv (1918) 184-
185. St James *N & Q* 12 ser v (1919) 174. St
Philip *N & Q* 12 ser iii (1917) 269. St Thomas
TS (1954-62). Sandhills Cmy *The "Sandhills".
An Historic Cemetery* by A. G. Foster (1918)
extr; *Gravestone Inscriptions of N.S.W.* Vol. I
by K. A. Johnson & M. R. Sainty (1973)
covers C of E, R.C., Presbyterian,
Congregational, Wesleyan Methodist, Jewish
Toganmaine *MIAu* 2
Vaucluse *MIAu* 2
Wollongong *Pioneer Park: The Old Church of
England Cemetery at Kembla and Bank
Streets, Wollongong 1848-1940* by A. P.
Fleming (1968)
NORTHERN TERRITORY Index of lone
graves Mfche of TS (c. 1976)
Darwin, Gardens Road Cmy Mfche of TS (c.
1980)
Katherine Cmy Mfche of TS (c. 1982)
QUEENSLAND Name index of persons buried
in Queensland cemeteries (Queensland F.H.S.
1983) microfilm
SOUTH AUSTRALIA Adelaide various TS
(1971)
TASMANIA *Gravely Tasmanian: A Friendly
Guide to Some Tasmanian Graveyards* by J. &
B. Emberg (1977-79) 3 vols
Hobart *Inscriptions in Stone: St David's Burial
Ground 1804-1872* by R. Lord (1976)
VICTORIA Ballarat, New Cmy MS (1955)
Bendigo, White Hills, General Cmy MS (1955)
Burwood, Pioneers B.g. *MIAu* 4
Camperdown Cmy MS (1933)
Chewton, General Cmy MS (1955)
Colac MS (c. 1955)
Cowes, Phillip Island MS (c. 1951)
Heidelberg, Public B.g. and small private cmy of
early pioneers *MIAu* 4
Melbourne, Fawkner Cmy MS (1955). General

Cmy extr *The Melbourne General Cemetery Centenary Souvenir* (1952). Old Cmy *MIAu* 4; *N & Q* 169 (1935) 346-348 386-387 456-457; 170 (1936) 118-119 153-154 206-207 261-262 314-315 404-405 457; 171 (1936) 61 277 419; 172 (1937) 62 208 282-283 351-352 442. St James *MIAu* 4

Oakleigh & Mulgrave, General Cmy *MIAu* 4

Wedderburn Cmy TS (1973)

WESTERN AUSTRALIA Australind TS (1967); extr TS (1967)

BELGIUM Bruges, Church of Capuchin Monks (one only) *Top & Gen* 2 (1853) 536. English Convent MS (1960). English Austin Nuns *Top & Gen* 2 (1853) 137-139 535 538. Notre Dame *ibid.* 139-140 468-470 537. St Croix (one only) *ibid.* 151 539. St Giles *ibid.* 535-536. General Cmy *ibid.* 140-151 537-538

Ghistelles, English Chyd *Misc Gen et Her* 3 ser v (1904) 266-267

Ostend, English Cmy *Misc Gen et Her* 3 ser v (1904) 261-266

CANADA

NOVA SCOTIA Annapolis, Fort Ann, Old B.g. *Misc Gen et Her* 4 ser i (1906) 153-154. Cmy *ibid* 4 ser ii (1908) 44-45

ONTARIO Adolphustown, South Fredericksburg and North Fredericksburg Cmys TS (1982)

Amherst Island: Glenwood Cmy TS (1980). Pentland Cmy TS (1980). St Bartholomew R.C. Cmy TS (1979)

Bedford, Thompson B.g. TS (1982)

Cataraqui, see Kingston

Hallowell township, Conger Cmy TS (1981)

Hinchinbrooke township, Piccadilly Cmy TS (1979)

Howe Island township, St Philomena R.C. Cmy TS (1975)

Kennebec township, Gaylord Cmy, Bordenwood Cmy, and Henderson United Church Cmy TS (1982)

Kingston township, Christ Church Cmy extr TS (1981). United Church Cmy TS (1982)

Leeds-Lansdowne townships, Herald Angel Anglican Church Cmy TS (1976)

Loughborough township, Desert Lake Cmy and Wilmer Cmy TS (1982)

Mackey Cmy TS (1976)

Murvale Cmy TS (1975)

Old Niagara Chyd *Misc Gen et Her* 2 ser v (1894) 373

Olden township, Oconto Cmy TS (1982)

Oso township, Christ Church Anglican Cmy TS

(1982). Zealand United Cmy TS (1982)

Pittsburgh township, Birmingham Mission TS (1983). Pine Grove Methodist Cmy TS (1976). Sand Hill Presbyterian Church Cmy TS (1976)

Portland township, Church of the Annunciation Cmy TS (1982). Verona Cmy TS (1979)

Port Stanley, Christ Church extr *Church in the Valley* by H. R. Rokeby-Thomas (1949) 46-47

Richmond Hill Cmy TS (1970)

Storrington township, Opinicon Cmy TS (1982)

Toronto, St Andrew Ch *Scottish Genealogist* 30:1 (1983) 18-23. Elia Church Cmy TS (1964)

Wolfe Island township, Sacred Heart R.C. Cmys, Old Cmy, New Cmy TS (1976, repr 1980). Christ Church Anglican Cmy TS (1972, repr 1980). Horne Cmy and Point Alexandra United Church Cmy TS (1973). St Lawrence United Church Cmy TS (1972, repr 1980). Trinity Church Anglican Cmy TS (1973, repr 1980)

QUEBEC Ayers Cliff, Brown's Hill Cmy MS (1961)

Gaspe, Forillon National Park (Channel Islands MI only) *Channel Islands Family History Journal* 17 (Winter 1982-83) 6-9; 18 (Spring 1983) 36-41

Georgeville, MacPherson Cmy MS (1961)

Sabrevois, Anglican Chyd TS (n.d.)

CEYLON *List of Inscriptions on Tombstones and Monuments in Ceylon* by J. Penry Lewis (1913)

CHILE Iquique *N & Q* 12 ser xii (1923) 27-28; *ibid* 165 (1933) 225-226

CHINA Canton, Shameen, Christ Church *N & Q* 12 ser xii (1923) 108-109

Macao Protestant Cmy MS (1920). *Tombstones in the English Cemeteries at Macao* by J. M. Braga (1940). Protestant Cmy & Seamen's Graves on Island of Kiau *Gen Mag* 8 (1938-39) 325-330

Peking, Old British Legation TS (1981)

CHRISTMAS ISLAND extr TS (1983)

CUBA Guantanamo Bay, U.S. Naval Cmy TS (1980)

CYPRUS Larnaca, Monastery of St George *N & Q* 10 ser vi (1906) 302-303. St Lazarus Chyd *ibid; Gwynedd Roots* (Journal of Gwynedd FHS) 11 (Nov 1986) 30-31

Omodos *N & Q* 10 ser vi (1906) 302-303

FALKLAND ISLAND DEPENDENCIES
South Georgia, South Shetland Islands &
Graham Land MS (1949)

FRANCE Avignon, Municipal Cmy (English)
N & Q 11 ser vii (1913) 26-27
Boulogne, Protestant Cmy *British Archivist* 1
(1913-14) 71-74 89-91
Caen, Protestant Cmy *Top & Gen* 2 (1853) 152;
Berks & Oxon MI by J. E. Bateson (1911) MS
Mentone, Ancien Cimetière *N & Q* 11 ser x
(1914) 326-327 383-384 464-465 504-505; xi
(1915) 85-86, index 205-206. Cimetière du
Chateau TS (1961)
Paris, Augustine Nunnery *Coll Top et Gen* 8
(1843) 24-31. Huguenot Cmy *Top & Gen* 3
(1857) 298-302 (copied 1675). Irish College
Coll Top et Gen 7 (1841) 111-117. Scotch
College *ibid* 32-42; Hearne VI, 332-333; VII,
110-111
War Graves *The War Graves of the British
Empire. France 550-556* (Imperial War Graves
Commission, 1928) Loos, Haisnes,
Mazingarbe, Grenay, Vermelles

GERMANY Bonn Old Cmy *Der Alte Friedhof
in Bonn* by E. Enne et al (1981) biographies of
Germans buried there
Dusseldorf, Dusselthal Cmy *Misc Gen et Her*
4 ser ii (1908) 251. Cmy on Golzheimer Insel
ibid. 247-249. Tannenwaldchen Cmy *ibid*.
250-251
Frankfurt Cmy *Misc Gen et Her* 3 ser iii (1900)
17-22 40-43. Jewish Cmy *ibid*. 43. St Peter
(one only) *ibid*. 17
Homberg, British subjects in various cmies *Misc
Gen et Her* 3 ser ii (1898) 164-175
Wiesbaden, Old Cmy *Misc Gen et Her* 2 ser v
(1894) 14-16, 3 ser i (1896) 152

GIBRALTAR Kings Chapel *N & Q* 11 ser ii
(1910) 342-344. Protestant Cathedral *N & Q*
11 ser iii (1911) 224-225. Sandpits Cmy *N & Q*
11 ser ii (1910) 423-425 483-484. Trafalgar
Cmy *N & Q* 11 ser i (1910) 104-105 165-166,
and index TS (n.d.); index TS (1986)

GREECE Athens, various crimes *Misc Gen et
Her* 3 ser iii (1900) 149-157 181-187. Cmy
(Protestant enclave) TS (1961)
Cephalonia (Kefalonia) British Cmy TS (1986)
Cerigo (Kithira), English Cmy *Misc Gen et Her*
4 ser iv (1912) 322-327
Corfu *Misc Gen et Her* 4 ser i (1906) 35-38 68-70
87-92 122-125 195-198 236-239 252-256 311-

312; ii (1908) 13-16 71-73 110-112 146-149 320-
321; 5 ser viii (1932-34) 85. *The Manchester
Genealogist* 13:3 (July 1977) 79. List
1892-1912 TS (n.d.)
Ithaca, British Cmy *Misc Gen et Her* 4 ser v
(1914) 177-179
Paxo, British Cmy *Misc Gen et Her* 4 ser ii
(1908) 321-322
Phalerum, Greek Cmy (English MI) *Misc Gen
et Her* 3 ser iii (1900) 286-290
Piraeus, Greek Cmy (English MI) *Misc Gen et
Her* 3 ser iii (1900) 285-286
Salonika, Protestant Cmy TS (1961)
Santa Maura, British Cmy *Misc Gen et Her*
4 ser ii (1908) 322-323
Zante, various *Misc Gen et Her* 4 ser v (1914)
19-27. St John's Cmy *Gen Mag* 7 (1935-37)
19-21

HONG KONG Happy Valley, Colonial Cmy
List Graves scheduled for removal 1863-1941
(1969); list of graves removed *Hong Kong
Gazette* no. 48 (1975) 3609-3695 (xerox)

INDIA
Anglo-Indian Collections by H. Bullock (1947)
TS. Anglo-Indian MI in and near Bath, and in
south Devon; ruinous graves notices in *The
Gazette of India;* MI from Banikhet,
Madhopur, Solan, Kasauli, Chamba, Aligarh,
Ghaziabad, Bahawalpur, Delhi St Mary RC;
extracts from Murray's *Handbook of Bengal
Presidency* (1882) — Agra, Morar, Muttra,
Aligarh, Moradabad, Naini Tal, Rangoon
(Burma), Hugli, Chinsura, Bandel, Serampur,
Bhagalpur, Monghyr, Bankipur, Patna, Gaya,
Arrah, Buxar, Darjeeling, Dacca, Benares;
Stray MI — Ceylon, Dutch East Indies,
Straits Settlements, Malaya, Indian Ocean,
Iran
An Indian Miscellany by H. Bullock & H. K.
Percy-Smith (1941-1944) TS. Benares, Persian
Gulf, Murree, Charial, Kuldana, Lower &
Upper Topa, Bilaspur, Delhi, Hansi, Harihar,
Mussoorie, Sirur, Chinsura, Dinapur, Meerut,
Rampur Boalia, Saugor, Anantapur district,
Chingleput district, Cuddapah district,
Kurnool district, Nellore district, North Arcot
district; and Urquart's *Oriental Obituary* vols.
1 & 3
'Monumental Inscriptions in India' by H.
Bullock printed in *Bengal Past and Present*
Vol. 41 (1931) 58-67 149-156 Naini Tal, Agra,
Sagauli (Bihar), Allahabad, Chunar, Nowgong
(CI)
Vol. 42 (1931) 1-17 MI in United Provinces

supplementing *The Bengal Obituary* (1851), Fuhrer (1896), Blunt (1911), and *Tombs and Monuments in charge of Public Works Dept, United Provinces* (Allahabad Government Press, 1913); 120-131 Murree, Poona, Kirkee, Ajaigarh (CI), Naini Tal, Ahmednagar, and a few elsewhere

Vol. 43 (1932) 92-109 Agra, Gwalior Rawalpindi, various Rajputana States, and a few elsewhere

Vol. 44 (1932) 169-175 Agra, Gwalior, Baroda, Jaipur, Loralai

Vol. 45 (1933) 44-59 Fort Sandeman, Ziarat (Baluchistan), Duki (Baluchistan), Karachi, and various from Hyderabad; 124-129 Hyderabad, Quetta, Pishin

Vol. 46 (1933) 74-90 Purnea, Fategarh

Vol. 49 (1935) 136-141 Anglo-Indian MI in Kent and Sussex

Vol. 50 (1935) 90-97 Anglo Indian MI in Kent and Sussex, Bhuj (Cutch)

Vol. 51 (1936) 105-111 Karachi, Murree Hills, Junagadh State, Hindubagh (Baluchistan)

Vol. 52 (1936) 105-112 Kathiawar various, Quetta, Attock (Punjab)

Vol. 53 (1937) 36-46 Sardhana (UP), Delhi, Murree Hills, Karnal, Campbellpur, Attock, and a few elsewhere; 89-99 Mahableshwar, Kukul (Hazara), Malakand, Haripur (Hazara), and a few elsewhere

Monumental Inscriptions in India Printed in "Bengal Past and Present" 1931-1937 by H. Bullock (1938) omnibus vol with cumulative index

Monumental Inscriptions – Miscellaneous by E. W. Topham-Steele, O. G. Knapp, et al. (1942) TS. Bihar — Sasarem, Segauli, Bhagalpur; Bombay Diocese — Fort Bombay, Colaba, Malabar Hill, Byculla, Thana, Lonavla, Kirkee, Poona, Satara, Purandhar, Mahableshwar, Castle Rock, Belgaum, Kolhapur, Deolali, Ahmednagar, Kaira, Baroda Camp, Surat, Broach, Rajkot, Mount Abu, Aden Crater, Steamer Point Aden; Kakul (UP); Erinpura & Udaipur (Rajputana)

ASSAM *List of Inscriptions on Tombs or Monuments in Assam* (1902)

BALUCHISTAN Bhag & Sibi *N & Q* 166 (1934) 151

Fort Sandeman *N & Q* 163 (1932) 365-366

Loralai *N & Q* 163 (1932) 205

Mach *N & Q* 166 (1934) 225

Mangi & Khost *N & Q* 166 (1934) 96

Nari Gorge *N & Q* 167 (1934) 26

Pishin & Hindubagh *N & Q* 164 (1933) 370-371

Quetta *N & Q* 164 (1933) 97-98

Sibi *N & Q* 166 (1934) 27

Ziarat & Duki *N & Q* 163 (1932) 349

See also PUNJAB

BENGAL *List of Inscriptions on Tombs or Monuments in Bengal* by C. R. Wilson (1896)

List of Old Inscriptions in Christian Burial Grounds in the Province of Bihar and Orissa (1926)

The Bengal Obituary: being MI from various parts of the Bengal and Agra Presidencies by Holmes and Co. (1851)

The Complete Monumental Register: epitaphs, inscriptions etc in churches and burial grounds in and about Calcutta by M. Derozario (1815). Includes various Calcutta B.gs; also Howrah, Dum-Dum, Barrasut, Barrackpore, Serampore, Chandernagore, Chinsurah, Convent of Bandel, and some from Madras, Bombay, Java, Penang, Isle of France

Calcutta Old Cmy *The East Indian Chronologist* (1801) 84-89. Old Cathedral *Illustrated Handbook to St John's Church (Old Cathedral) Calcutta* (1909). South Park Street Cmy *The South Park Street Cemetery* by H. Holloway & M. Shellim (1978). French Cmy *French Cemetery, Park Street* by B. Labouchardiere (1983)

Patna *List of Pre-Mutiny Inscriptions in Christian Burial Grounds in the Patna District* (1936). Catholic Church *A Record of the Inscriptions at the Catholic Church at Patna* by A. Gille (1917)

Puri *Inscriptions in the District of Puri* by W. H. Lee (1898)

Purnea *N & Q* 165 (1933) 149-152 166-168 187-188

Sagauli *N & Q* 160 (1931) 79

Serampore, Mission B.g. *Bengal Past and Present* 47 (1934) 57-65

BENGAL, EAST Dacca Cmy *Bengal Past and Present* 31 (1926) 10-12

BERAR see CENTRAL PROVINCES

BOMBAY *Revised List of Tombs and Monuments in Bombay and other parts of the Presidency* (1912)

Bhuj *N & Q* 168 (1935) 273-274 308-309

Gogho *N & Q* 168 (1935) 384-385

Junagadh *N & Q* 166 (1934) 277-278; 168 (1935) 224

Kaira Chyd MS (1968)

Karachi *N & Q* 163 (1932) 420-423; 170 (1936) 333 416-419

Kirkee *N & Q* 161 (1931) 332-333

Poona, East Street Cmy *N & Q* 161 (1931) 297-298

Porbandur *British Archivist* 1 (1913) 82 (bound with *Monumental Inscriptions* by E. W. Topham-Steele et al). *N & Q* 169 (1935) 27

Rajkot *N & Q* 169 (1935) 168-170
Surat *An Account of the Old Tombs in the Cemeteries of Surat* by A. F. Bellasis (1861) repr from *Journal of the Bombay Branch of the Royal Asiatic Society* vol. 6, p. 146 with some alterations
BUNDELKHAND *N & Q* 160 (1931) 259; 161 (1931) 317
CENTRAL INDIA see RAJPUTANA
CENTRAL PROVINCES *List of Inscriptions on Tombs or Monuments in the Central Provinces and Berar* (1932)
DELHI see PUNJAB
FRENCH POSSESSIONS see MADRAS
GWALIOR *N & Q* 160 (1931) 455; 162 (1932) 260
HYDERABAD *List of Inscriptions on Tombs or Monuments in H. E. H. The Nizam's Dominions* by O. S. Crofton (1941). See also MADRAS and (for Berar) CENTRAL PROVINCES
INDORE Mandleshwar & Mehidpur *N & Q* 160 (1931) 455
KASHMIR see PUNJAB
MADRAS *List of Inscriptions on Tombs or Monuments in Madras* by J. J. Cotton (1905). (Revised edn in 2 vols 1945-46). Includes also Fort Marlborough (Sumatra), French India, Travancore, Mysore and Hyderabad
European and Eurasian Tombs: Kistna, North Arcot, Vizagapatam, Bellary, Godaveri, Coimbatore, Ganjam (1893-95) omnibus vol
Fort St George *A Handbook to St Mary's Church, Fort St George, Madras* by C. H. Malden (1905). *St Mary's Church, Fort St George, Madras 1680-1953* by W. H. Warren & N. Barlow (1953)
MYSORE Seringapatam *A Handbook for the use of visitors to Seringapatam* by V. C. Subbaraya Moodeliar (1907) appendix Z. See also MADRAS
PUNJAB *A List of Inscriptions on Christian Tombs or Monuments in the Punjab, North-West Frontier Province, Kashmir and Afghanistan* by M. Irving (1910)
Supplementary List of Inscriptions on Tombs or Monuments in the Punjab, North-West Frontier Province, Kashmir, Sind, Afghanistan and Baluchistan by H. L. O. Garrett (1935)
Attock Fort *N & Q* 171 (1936) 386
Campbellpur *N & Q* 171 (1936) 454-455
Delhi, European Cmy, Kashmir Gate TS (1985)
Gharial *N & Q* 170 (1936) 456
Jhelum, Dina Camping Ground *N & Q* 172 (1937) 316
Jullundur & Karnal *N & Q* 172 (1937) 117

Kuldana *N & Q* 171 (1936) 94-95
Rawalpindi *N & Q* 162 (1932) 98
Simla, Chota Simla or Mall, Cart Road, Park, and Sanjauli *Simla Genealogical Collections* by H. Bullock (1946) TS
Sohan *N & Q* 172 (1937) 316
Upper Topa *N & Q* 171 (1936) 294
RAJPUTANA and CENTRAL INDIA *List of Inscriptions on Tombs or Monuments in Rajputana and Central India* by O. S. Crofton (1934)
Erinpura *British Archivist* 1 (1913) 30-31 (bound with *Monumental Inscriptions* by E. W. Topham-Steele et al)
SIND see BOMBAY and PUNJAB
TRAVANCORE see MADRAS
UNITED PROVINCES *List of Christian Tombs and Monuments in the North-Western Provinces and Oudh* by A. Fuhrer (1896)
List of Inscriptions on Christian Tombs and Tablets in the United Provinces of Agra and Oudh by E. A. H. Blunt (1911)
Allahabad, Muir Road Cmy in vol entitled *Miscellaneous 1948* by H. Bullock (1949) TS
Benares, St Mary's Church, Indian Cmy, and Chouka Ghat Cmy *Heritage* (Journal of Windsor, Slough and District F.H.S.) 2:2-4 (1979); 3:1-4 (1979/80)
Cawnpore, Memorial Church *Key to the Tablets in the Memorial Church, Cawnpore 1857* by R. MacCrea (1893). Cantonment Cmy *Misc Gen et Her* 4 ser i (1906) 54-56 114-119 142-145 172-176 216-219 257-261 294-296; ii (1908) 21-23 61-64 138-139 164-165. Kacheri Cmy *A Guide to the Kacheri Cemetery and the Early History of Kanpur* by Z. Yalland (1983); *Kacheri Cemetery, Kanpur* by Z. Yalland (1985)
Chunar *N & Q* 160 (1931) 151
Fategarh *N & Q* 165 (1933) 5-8
Haripur *N & Q* 172 (1937) 207 316
Kakul *N & Q* 172 (1937) 296
Malakand *N & Q* 172 (1937) 260
Mardan, Guides Cmy *N & Q* 172 (1937) 316
Naini Tal, St John in the Wilderness *N & Q* 159 (1930) 456-458; 160 (1931) 6-7
see also BENGAL and PUNJAB

INDONESIA see SUMATRA

IRAN Akbarabad, Protestant Cmy MS (1974)
Bassadore, British Cmy *N & Q* 174 (1938) 148-149

ITALY Alassio *N & Q* 11 ser xi (1915) 296-297
Bellagio, English Cmy *N & Q* 10 ser xi (1909)

325. Foreign Cmy *N & Q* 10 ser vii (1907) 164-165

Cadennabbia & Griante Ch & Campo Santo Cmy *N & Q* 10 ser vi (1906) 446; 11 ser x (1914) 407. Little Cmy *Misc Gen et Her* 2 ser iii (1890) 202-203

Capri *N & Q* 10 ser v (1906) 381-382

Cava dei Tirreni *N & Q* 10 ser vi (1906) 406

Florence, Old Protestant Cmy *N & Q* 10 ser ix (1908) 224-225 344-345 443-445; x (1908) 24-26 223-224 324-325 463-464. New Protestant Cmy *N & Q* 11 ser iii (1911) 324-325 404-405

Leghorn, Old Protestant Cmy *Misc Gen et Her* 3 ser ii (1898) 88-90 113-116 149-152 178-184; iv (1902) 31-35 66-70 99-103 133-137, printed as *The Inscriptions in the Old British Cemetery of Leghorn* by G. M. G. Cullum & F. C. Macauley (1906)

Milan, Protestant Cmy *N & Q* 10 ser vi (1906) 4-5

Naples, Old Protestant Cmy *N & Q* 10 ser viii (1907) 62-63 161-163 242-244 362-363 423-425. New Protestant Cmy *N & Q* 10 ser xii (1909) 303 362-363. Catholic Cmy *ibid* 363

Palermo, Old Protestant Cmy *Misc Gen et Her* 2 ser v (1894) 327-329 337-338; TS (1964). New Protestant Cmy TS (1964)

Rome, English College *Coll Top et Gen* v (1838) 87-88. Protestant Cmy (Americans & Canadians only) *North American Records in Italy: The Protestant Cemetery of Rome* by R. R. & R. K. Stevens (1981)

Sorrento Cmy *N & Q* 10 ser vi (1906) 406

Venice, Old Protestant Cmy *Misc Gen et Her* 2 ser i (1886) 347-348

KOREA Seoul & others *Yanghwajin Seoul Foreigners' Cemetery, Korea with notes on other Foreign Cemeteries in Korea* by D. N. Clark (1984)

MALAYSIA Georgetown (Penang) Northam Road Cmy TS (1974)

Kota Kinabalu (Jesselton) TS (1980)

Labuan, Old Naval Cmy MS (1925)

Malacca, Christ Church TS (1974); *Christian Cemeteries and Memorials in Malacca* by A. Harfield (1984). St Paul Ch & Chyd TS (1974); Harfield *op. cit.* Fort Cmy Harfield *op. cit.* Portuguese & Dutch MI *Historical Tombstones of Malacca* by R. N. Bland (1904); Harfield *op. cit.*

Sabah & Sandakan, Old European Cmy TS (1980)

Sarawak, Kuching TS (1956). Miri TS (1957)

MALTA Msida Bastion Cmy TS (1930)

Pieta, Ta Braxia Cmy TS (1977)

Valletta, St John *The Church of St John in Valletta* by Sir H. P. Scicluna (1955) appendix

MEXICO Real Del Monte, English Cmy list TS (n.d.)

NEPAL Kathmandu, British Cmy TS (n.d.); & photos

NEW ZEALAND Canterbury, Brackenbridge R.C. Cmy TS (1972)

Christchurch, Barbadoes Street Cmy TS (1973)

Scottish graves at Reefton, Auckland, Milton, Dunedin, Wellington, Timaru, Christchurch, Lyttleton in *Aberdeen & North-Scotland FHS Newsletter* 15 (June 1985) 7-9; 18 (Spring 1986) 7-8

PAKISTAN Dacca see INDIA, BENGAL EAST

Karachi see INDIA general & BOMBAY

PALESTINE Jerusalem *Misc Gen et Her* 3 ser iv (1902) 44-48 86-89. *N & Q* 10 ser xi (1909) 25 163-165

PERSIAN GULF see INDIA general

PORTUGAL Lisbon, British Cmy TS (1939) copied 1825; TS (1943); West Country names *Devon N & Q* 22 (1942-46) 364-368; extr *Avon Monumental Inscriptions* 6 (1978-79) MS

RUSSIA *Memorials of the Brave; or Resting Places of our Fallen Heroes in the Crimea and at Scutari* by J. Colborne & F. Brine (1857, 2nd edn 1858)

ST HELENA *N & Q* 175 (1938) 258-259 300-301. St James, Jamestown Ch MS (1956); Chyd TS (1986). St Peter TS (1986). St Paul TS (1986)

SARAWAK see MALAYSIA

SAUDI ARABIA Jedda *N & Q* 168 (1935) 326-329 332-333 344-348 363-365; 173 (1937) 62-64

SINGAPORE Fort Canning Cmy TS (1978)

SPAIN Malaga, Protestant Cmy *N & Q* 11 ser i (1910) 444-445 502-503
Minorca, Mahon, San Felipe Protestant Cmy TS (1932); *Gen Mag* 6 (1933) 214
San Sebastian, Monte Urgull Cmy *N & Q* 10 ser iii (1905) 361
Tenerife, Las Palmas, English Cmy *N & Q* 10 ser i (1904) 483-485, ii (1905) 155; Spanish Cmy *N & Q* 10 ser i (1904) 482-483. Orotava, All Saints Ch MS (1972); English Cmy *N & Q* 10 ser i (1904) 361-362 455, ii (1905) 155; MS (1978). Santa Cruz, English Cmy *N & Q* 10 ser i (1904) 442-443

SUMATRA Bencoolen and Fort Marlborough *Bencoolen. The Christian Cemetery and the Fort Marlborough Monuments* by A. Harfield (1985); *Gen Mag* 8 (1939) 383-385. Fort Marlborough TS (1986). See also INDIA, MADRAS

SWITZERLAND Aigle, English Cmy MS (c. 1950), Index TS (1969)
Berne, Bremgarten Chyd & Cmy, Monbijou Cmy, Rosengarten Cmy, Schosshalden Cmy *Misc Gen et Her* 3 ser ii (1898) 2-6
Chareau d'Oex (Vaud) MS (n.d.)
Clarens, All Saints English Cmy MS (c. 1950), Index TS (1969)
Geneva, Petit Saconnex Cmy *N & Q* 10 ser xii (1909) 183-184
Interlaken, Chyd *N & Q* 171 (1936) 95-96
Leysin, English Cmy MS (c. 1950), Index TS (1969)
Lucerne, Kreuzbuch English Cmy *N & Q* 10 ser vi (1906) 124-126 195. Kreuzbuch English Cmy, St Mark's Church, Old Cmy, Town (New) Cmy *Misc Gen et Her* 3 ser iv (1902) 118-121 156-159
Montreux, Cmy *N & Q* 171 (1936) 96
Ouchy, Cmy *Misc Gen et Her* 3 ser ii (1898) 102-104
Pontresina, Santa Maria Chyd *N & Q* 13 ser i (1923) 268-269
Sallaz (near Lausanne) *Misc Gen et Her* 3 ser i (1896) 243-246
Samaden, English Church Chyd *N & Q* 13 ser i (1923) 349-350
Schaffhausen *Misc Gen et Her* 3 ser iv (1902) 159
Territet, New Cmy MS (c. 1950), Index TS (1969)
Vevey, English Cmy MS (c. 1950), Index TS (1969)
Veytaux, English Cmy MS (c. 1950), Index TS (1969)

Villeneure, English Cmy MS (c. 1950), Index TS (1969)
Zermatt, Village Cmy & English Ch & Chyd MS (1949)

SYRIA Aleppo, Old Protestant Cmy *N & Q* 11 ser xi (1915) 101-102; TS (1954)

THAILAND Chiangmai *De Mortuis: The Story of the Chiang Mai Foreign Cemetery 1898-1980* by R. W. Wood (1980) biographies of persons buried there, not actual MI

TURKEY Alexandretta, Mariakoudi Chyd *N & Q* 11 ser xii (1915) 93-94. Vicinity of Greek Orthodox Church *Gen Mag* ix (1945) 469-471
Angora *N & Q* 11 ser xii (1915) 94
Constantinople, Pera MS (1859), also incomplete TS with index (1919)
Smyrna, Old Cmy *N & Q* 11 ser xii (1915) 62
See also RUSSIA

UNITED STATES OF AMERICA
CALIFORNIA Dixon Cmy TS (1935)
Antioch, Rose Hill Cmy TS (1979)
MASSACHUSETTS Boston *The Graveyards of Boston: First Volume, Copp's Hill Epitaphs* by W. H. Whitmore (1878)
Plymouth *Handbook of Old Burial Hill, Plymouth* by F. H. Perkins (1947). *Epitaphs from Burial Hill, Plymouth from 1657 to 1892* by B. Kingman (repr 1977)
NEVADA Aurora Cmy TS (1966)
NEW YORK *Between the Lakes Cemeteries* by C. W. Fischer & H. J. Swick (1974) 3 vols. Portions of Seneca, Schuyler & Tompkins counties
New York, Trinity *Churchyards of Trinity Parish in the City of New York 1697-1947* no author (1955); *Churchyards of Trinity Parish in the City of New York 1697-1969* by J. V. Butler (1969)
North Tarrytown *The Old Dutch Burying Ground of Sleepy Hollow* (History Research Soc. of Tappan Zee, 1926). *The Old Dutch Burying Ground of Sleepy Hollow in North Tarrytown* by W. G. Perry (1953)
WASHINGTON *Naselle to Grays River and Knappton to Nemah, Washington Cemetery Records and Genealogical Notes* by R. E. Yancy (1978) Boldt (Pillar Rock), Grays River Grange, Deep River, Eden Valley, Elliott

(Dahlia), Jones (Altoona), Nemah, New Salmon Creek, Knappton, Old Salmon Creek, Peaceful Hill Naselle, Old Grays River, Rosburg, Smith Island, Seal River, Upper Naselle-Kainber, Walker (Grays River), and miscellaneous

URUGUAY Montevideo, Busceo, Royal Naval Graves TS (n.d.)

WEST INDIES
Monumental Inscriptions of the British West Indies by J. H. Lawrence-Archer (1875). Antigua, Barbados, British Guiana, Jamaica, St Kitts, Nevis & Anguilla
Papers relating to the Preservation of Historic Sites & Monuments & Buildings in the West Indian Colonies (H.M.S.O. 1912). Barbados, British Guiana, Dominica etc
The Monumental Inscriptions of the British West Indies by V. L. Oliver (1927). Antigua, Bahamas, Demerara, Dominica, Grenada, Montserrat, Nevis, St Kitts, St Lucia, Tobago, Trinidad, naval & military b.gs.
For MI in England relating to West Indies see *Caribbeana* 1-5 (1910-1919)
ANTIGUA English Harbour Military B.g. *N & Q* 10 ser v (1906) 62-63
BAHAMAS Nassau, Christ Church MS (1938). St Matthew's Cmy & Eastern B.g. microfiche of Kent F.H.S. Record Publication no. 243 (1986)
BARBADOS "Monumental Inscriptions of Barbados" in *Gent Mag* (1863) II, 426-434 567-575. Christ Church, St Andrew, St James, St John, St Joseph, St Lucy, St Michael Cathedral, St Peter, St Philip, St Thomas
The Monumental Inscriptions in the Churches & Churchyards of the Island of Barbados by V. L. Oliver (1915). St Michael Cathedral; Bridgetown St Leonard, St Paul, & St Mary; Military B.g., Nedham's Point; The Savannah of St Ann; St Michael; Christ Church; St Matthias; St George; St James, Hole Town; St Peter, Speights Town; All Saints Chapel, St Peter's; St Philip; St Thomas; St Joseph; St Andrew; St John; St Ann; Jewish B.g., Bridgetown
Bridgetown, Jewish B.g. *Monumental Inscriptions in the Burial Ground of the Jewish Synagogue at Bridgetown, Barbados* by E. M. Shilstone (1956). Copy by V. L. Oliver *supra* also printed in *Transactions of the Jewish Historical Society of England* 13 (1932-35) 97-108
Nedham's Point, Naval & Military Cmy *N & Q* 12 ser x (1922) 23-25 46-47
St Michael, Cathedral *Journal of the Barbados Museum & Historical Society* 15:2 (Feb 1948) 103-105; 30:4 (May 1964) 183-185
St Paul *N & Q* 155 (1928) 42-43
GRENADA St George Ch & Chyd *Journal of the Barbados Museum & Historical Society* 16:3 (May 1949) 118-127
JAMAICA "Monumental Inscriptions of Jamaica" in *Gent Mag* (1864) I, 42-49 182-189 595-605. Clarendon, Falmouth, Kingston, Montego Bay, Spanish Town, St Andrew, Vere, and various private b.gs.
Monumental Inscriptions of Jamaica by P. Wright (1966). Kingston, St Andrew, St Catherine, Clarendon, Manchester, St Elizabeth, Westmoreland, Hanover, St James, Trelawny, St Ann, St Mary, Portland, St Thomas
TS (n.d.) Clarks Town (Trelawny), Falmouth (Trelawny), Lucea (Hanover), Montego Bay, Maroons Town, Cinammon Hill
Kingston, Jewish Cmy *N & Q* 10 ser xii (1909) 105-106
St Thomas, Golden Grove Cmy *Gen Mag* 20 (1980) 17 (additional to those in P. Wright *supra*)
Salt River *Caribbeana* 4 (1916) 48
Spanish Town, Cathedral Ch & Chyd *Caribbeana* 1 (1910) 213-219 278-284 (annotations to Lawrence-Archer *supra*)
Vere *Historic Jamaica* by F. Cundall (1915) 387-392 (also a few from other parishes *passim*)
NEVIS St George *Caribbeana* 2 (1912) 314
St John Fig Tree *Caribbeana* 1 (1910) 45
St Paul *Caribbeana* 2 (1912) 168
St Thomas Lowland *Caribbeana* 2 (1912) 355
ST KITTS St Thomas, Middle Island *Caribbeana* 2 (1912) 204
Trinity, Palmetto Point *Caribbeana* 2 (1912) 358

YUGOSLAVIA Belgrade *Misc Gen et Her* 3 ser i (1896) 192